THE PEOPLE OF THE ABYSS

JACK LONDON

THE PEOPLE OF OF THE ABYSS

Introduction
by
JACK LINDSAY

The Journeyman Press, London

First published in Great Britain 1903
New edition by the Journeyman Press 1977
Reprinted in present format, 1978, 1980, 1981
97 Ferme Park Road, Crouch End, London N8 9SA and
17 Old Mill Road, West Nyack, NY 10994

Introduction © by Jack Lindsay, 1977

ISBN 0 904526 17 8

Other *Journeyman* Jack London

The Iron Heel, his famous novel about
America in the grip of big business and the military

Revolution: Stories and Essays, a new selection of his
best short stories and socialist essays
by Robert Barltrop

*All three books are available in an
attractive slip-cased edition*

Printed in Great Britain

CONTENTS

Chapter

	List of Illustrations	1
	Introduction by Jack Lindsay	3
	Preface	9
1	The Descent	11
2	Johnny Upright	16
3	My Lodging and Some Others	18
4	A Man and the Abyss	20
5	Those on the Edge	25
6	Frying-pan Alley and a Glimpse of Inferno	29
7	A Winner of the Victoria Cross	33
8	The Carter and the Carpenter	35
9	The Spike	42
10	Carrying the Banner	51
11	The Peg	53
12	Coronation Day	60
13	Dan Cullen, Docker	67
14	Hops and Hoppers	70
15	The Sea Wife	75
16	Property *v.* Persons	77
17	Inefficiency	80
18	Wages	84
19	The Ghetto	87
20	Coffee-houses and Doss-houses	95
21	The Precariousness of Life	100
22	Suicide	106
23	The Children	110
24	A Vision of the Night	113
25	The Hunger Wail	115
26	Drink, Temperance and Thrift	120
27	The Management	124

LIST OF ILLUSTRATIONS

facing page

1	In Wapping	18
2	A small Doss House	19
3	Spitalfields Garden	32
4	The Poplar Workhouse	33
5	The "Spike" – waiting outside Whitechapel Workhouse	44
6	Casual Ward, Whitechapel Workhouse	45
7	The Salvation Army Barracks – waiting	56
8	Salvation Army Barracks – in the Courtyard	57

INTRODUCTION

JACK LONDON was the first industrial worker to depict his world fully in words, to strive to understand it to its depths, and to express in novel, short story, speech, and essay the struggles of his fellows with powerful realism and a revolutionary perspective. The only other writer with whom we can compare him is Gorky; but Gorky's world was largely one of peasant and craftsman. What both men shared was a dogged determination to face the facts of their societies and follow them out to their final consequences. London admired Gorky and wrote an essay in praise of him in 1907.

He had some capable predecessors in dealing with the American scene, such as Crane and Norris; but he alone grasped the full nature of what was going on, and was able to relate particular manifestations of the system to the whole, shedding all illusions and realising clearly the direction in which society was moving.

Born on January 12, 1876 in San Francisco, he had an astrologer as father and a spiritualist as mother; but while he was still a baby, his mother married a migrant worker. There was a bad depression and the family kept moving, turning to job after job. From the outset there was never the least security. When Jack was a boy, they spent three years on a desolate ranch in dire poverty. 'I had never had toys nor plaything like other children. The pinch of poverty became chronic. And only a child, with a child's imagination, can come to know the meaning of things it has long been denied.'

There he defines the dual impulse that drove him on all his life, begetting deep contradictions and in the end tearing him to pieces: a determination to share in the good things of the world, and a sense of exclusion that brought him to a revolutionary position. One part of him wanted desperately to rise in the world; another part of him wanted to ensure that all the oppressed and deprived people, in America and everywhere else, had their full share in the enjoyment of the earth.

In the world of bitter hardship where he grew up, he had to be ready to take up whatever chance of a job was offered. He delivered newspapers out of school hours, bought an old boat and came to know every cranny of the San Francisco waterfront, every way of picking up an odd cent there. When he left school at thirteen, he worked in a cannery, then became a desperate oyster-pirate and a hard drinker. Turning patrol officer for a while, he shipped on a boat for Japan, hunted seals, worked in a jute-mill amid another harsh depression, and finally gained some encouragement for his struggles to write down the things he saw and experienced, by winning a newspaper prize with an essay on a typhoon. Working now in a power plant, he ambitiously took on two jobs and found that one of the displaced men committed suicide.

3

This was a crucial moment. He quit his job and tried to join in one of the great marches of the unemployed across America in support of a bill for a nationwide road-building programme. The year was 1894 and Jack was eighteen years old. He already had had some experience of tramping; two years before he had walked across the Sierras to Nevada and back, winning the nickname of Sailor Kid. Now he made his way east as best he could: in boxcars, on coach-roofs, even in the ice-box of a refrigerator car, at times exposed to snow-blizzards, dodging brakemen and nearly freezing to death. Once 'it took half an hour's brisk walk to restore circulation'. All the while he was half-starving and the problem of keeping up with the march was insuperable. As a hobo he rode the rails to Chicago, then to New York, begging, sleeping in fields, barns, boxcar. At Niagara Falls he was jailed as a vagrant for thirty days, and saw how the prisoners were robbed, beaten to death, tortured. Free, he hopped the cars of the Canadian Pacific and made his way back to the west coast.

A new Jack London emerged. He had learned of working-class organisation, of Marx and Socialism. At this moment the American socialist movement was growing fast, no longer a matter of scattered groups but with a national organisation that owned a chain of newspapers and magazines. Jack got hold of a copy of *The Communist Manifesto*, which he eagerly studied and absorbed. It provided the basic structure of understanding which he filled out from his own rich experiences. He became quickly a first-class debater and outdoor speaker.

Going to the Klondyke where gold had been struck, he mined no gold, but enlarged his knowledge of men and the world. He worked his way back home as a stoker. Then he washed windows and at last had a story of his accepted. His career as a writer had begun. He did his best to equip himself intellectually by reading as widely as he could, taking to Hegel, Spencer, Darwin, Huxley, but particularly affected by Marx and Nietzsche. Certain reactionary streaks, gained in his early years, persisted despite his passionate adherence to socialism. He kept a fixed belief in white supremacy and was aghast in 1905 that a 'yellow, inferior race' like the Japanese could defeat the Russians. Yet he could write enthusiastically of Japanese socialists and their declaration that 'for us Socialists there are no boundaries, race, country or nationality,' while maintaining, 'I am first of all a white man, and only then a Socialist'. He also had backward views on women.

Once he had begun as a writer he threw himself into the production of books with all his incredible energy. While strenuously advocating socialism and never sparing himself as a propagandist, he built up a private fortune so that he could live in a fine mansion, with a ship of his own, and so on. In his writing he mixed hack fiction with masterpieces. Among the latter were works like *The People of the Abyss*, with its terrible and sustained picture of working-class conditions in London; works like *The Call of the*

Wild and *White Fang*, in which his own experience of extreme hardship and endurance, of survival under shattering conditions, gave him a deep insight into wild animal life.

The same elements lay behind his *Martin Eden*, a remarkable account of a worker educating himself under crushing difficulties, in which both his socialist passion and his strong vein of individualism asserted themselves. Here, as in the powerfully dramatic *Sea Wolf*, he showed how individualism as a sheer unadulterated force destroyed itself; and he complained that socialist critics failed to see his aim—though in neither work does he give a glimpse of the counter-force, the struggle for socialism, which in fact consumed him.

In 1907, partly inspired by the brutal suppression of the 1905 Revolution, he wrote his great work, *The Iron Heel*, in which, with immense force and deep insight, he expressed his conviction that the capitalists would use every device of fraud and violence to hold their positions. He thus, in effect, wrote a penetrating prophecy of fascism.

He himself sailed off in his own ship in what was meant to be a seven-year pleasure-trip but which was soon ended through his illness. In the South Seas he took part in blackbirding, the cruel kidnapping of natives for slave-labour. More and more he grew sick of the need to keep on churning out work for money. Ironically, his magnificent Wolf House, costing some 70,000 dollars, was burnt down the night after its completion.

He defended American intervention across the Mexican border. The almost unbelievable contradictions in his mind are shown by the fact that in October 1913 he called on young men never to enter the army. 'Down with the army and the navy. We don't need killing institutions. We need life-giving institutions.' Then in 1914 he uncritically supported the Allies against Germany when war broke out. He had left the Socialist Party because it was full of compromise; now in this important matter he sided with the compromisers. On November 22, 1916 he killed himself with an overdose of morphine.

His daughter summed up: 'He was a more tragic sell-out, for he had been subsidised, bought body and soul, by the kind of life he thought he wanted, and it was destroying him.' That was true, and yet there was his deeper other side: the man selflessly devoted to the revolution and the cause of the common people, who owned unparalleled insights into the lot of the working class and the nature of capitalism. The intensity and the whole-heartedness with which he threw himself into his activities were reflected in the powerfully direct and sinewy style with which he depicted event, situation, character. And his writings were at once recognised by his fellow-workers as their own, and were read by millions. With all its strange contradictions his work remains a great achievement, an enduring monument of working-class struggle at a crucial moment of world development.

The two works in which he most fully uttered his socialist faith and integrated his vision were *The Iron Heel* and *The People of the Abyss*. In 1902 he had been commissioned by the American Press Association to go out to South Africa and write an account of the way things had worked out after the Boer War. But instead of going there directly he sailed to England. He had thought it would be a good idea to break his journey for two days in London, during which he would watch the coronation of Edward VII and report it from a socialist viewpoint. However the South African project was suddenly cancelled, and so he turned to an idea that he had tentatively discussed with an American publisher: an account of the London slums. For seven weeks he wandered round East London, talking to the people, living as they did, probing thoroughly into the conditions of their lives. Never had he been so completely absorbed in an experience. On August 25, 1902 he wrote to Anna Strunsky, 'I was out all night with the homeless ones, walking the streets in the bitter rain, and, drenched to the skin, wondering when dawn would come. Sunday I spent with the homeless ones, in the fierce struggle for something to eat. I returned to my rooms Sunday evening after thirty-six hours continuous work and a short one night's sleep . . . I am worn out and exhausted and my nerves are blunted with what I have seen and the suffering it has cost me'. His friend Upton Sinclair reported that 'for years afterwards the memories of this stunted and depraved population haunted him beyond all peace'. He himself declared, 'No other book of mine took so much of my young heart and tears as that study of the economic degradation of the poor'.

Back in the States, London placed his account with a socialist periodical, *Wilshire's Magazine,* which had only a small circulation. But the work had a rapid success. Previously known mainly to the socialists of the west coast, London now became a national figure. His story ran as a serial from March 1903 to January 1904, but already in November 1903 Macmillan published it in book form and four months later an English edition appeared from Pitman. In 1903 *The Call of the Wild*, a story of a dog which after its master's death joins a wolfpack, also appeared, and London was launched on his career as a highly successful and well-paid author.

In a way it was nothing new for a writer to make a journey into slumland and return to recount its horrors. The Victorians had been both fascinated with the lowlife of the slums and terrified of the slum-denizens. It is hard for us to realise how completely clothes, manners, talk, attitudes to every aspect of life divided the people of England into two nations; and the middle-class person who ventured into the jungle of lowlife felt like an explorer in darkest Africa. Not for nothing had William Booth, founder of the Salvation Army, called his book on the slums *In Darkest England and the Way Out* (1890). Asking 'Why Darkest England,' he gave an account of Stanley in the Congo and went on, 'As there is a darkest Africa, is there not also a darkest England?' Englishmen could 'discover within a stone's throw of our cathedrals and palaces similar horrors to those which Stanley has found existing in the great Equatorial forest.' George R. Sims, a capable journalist, remarked in his *How the Poor Live and Horrible London* (1889) of the perils of his journey into East London: 'It is unpleasant to be mistaken, in underground cellars where the vilest outcasts hide from the light of day, for detectives in search of their prey—it is dangerous to breathe for some hours at a stretch an atmosphere charged with infection and poisoned with indescribable effluvia—it is hazardous to be hemmed in down a blind alley by a crowd of roughs who have had hereditarily transmitted to them the maxim of John Leech, that half-bricks were specially designed for the benefit of 'strangers'.' He too fell back on the comparison with savage tribes,

> It is to increased wealth and to increased civilisation that we owe the wide gulf which today separates well-to-do citizens from the masses. It is the increased wealth of this mighty city which has driven the poor back inch by inch, until we find them today herding together, packed like herrings in a barrel, neglected and despised, and left to endure wrongs and hardships which, if they were related of a far-off savage tribe, would cause Exeter Hall to shudder till its bricks fell down . . . They have become natural curiosities, and to this fact they may owe the honour in store for them, of dividing public attention with the Senanas, the Aborigines, and the South Sea Islanders.

London in his book also used the analogy with tribal folk, but in order to make a different point. He compared the British poor with the Indians of Alaska. Among the Innuit on the banks of the Yukon River, he pointed out, chronic starvation was unknown; for the people shared out what they had. If things were short, they all suffered; when there was plenty, they all ate their fill. Only in the civilised world did men starve in the midst of plenty, with one man living in a fine mansion while another slept in a dark doorway.

But while works like those of William Booth and Sims, of Mayhew and James Greenwood, and many others, did a certain service in drawing attention to the lot of the poor and at times gave striking accounts of how terrible that lot was, there was a wholly new quality in London's book. The reviewer in *The Independent* at the time brought out the essential point. 'This life has been pictured many times before—complacently by Professor A. Wyckoff, luridly by Mr. Stead, scientifically by Mr Charles Booth. But Mr. London alone has made it real and present to us.' However genuine the humanitarian feeling of the others, none of them could truly identify himself with the workers and feel them as human beings. London took as much care to get his details correct as did say Charles Booth with his *Life and Labour of the People in London* (1889 and 1891), to depict the slum-scene just as it was in all its crude facts; but at the same time he realised the outcast people as his

7

brothers and sisters, as himself, without letting any sentimentality blur his vision. He could thus enter with his whole being into the situations and comprehend them from inside as well as depicting them vividly from outside. The result is a passionate document, historically valid and yet as vitally alive as any deeply imaginative novel could be. For us, as for his readers of 1903, he makes the life of the East London masses 'real and present'.

JACK LINDSAY

PREFACE

THE experiences related in this volume fell to me in the summer of 1902. I went down into the under-world of London with an attitude of mind which I may best liken to that of the explorer. I was open to be convinced by the evidence of my eyes, rather than by the teachings of those who had not seen, or by the words of those who had seen and gone before. Further, I took with me certain simple criteria with which to measure the life of the under-world. That which made for more life, for physical and spiritual health, was good; that which made for less life, which hurt, and dwarfed, and distorted life, was bad.

It will be readily apparent to the reader that I saw much that was bad. Yet it must not be forgotten that the time of which I write was considered 'good times' in England. The starvation and lack of shelter I encountered constituted a chronic condition of misery which is never wiped out, even in the periods of greatest prosperity.

Following the summer in question came a hard winter. Great numbers of the unemployed formed into processions, as many as a dozen at a time, and daily marched through the streets of London crying for bread. Mr. Justin McCarthy, writing in the month of January 1903, to the New York *Independent*, briefly epitomizes the situation as follows:

'The workhouses have no space left in which to pack the starving crowds who are craving every day and night at their doors for food and shelter. All the charitable institutions have exhausted their means in trying to raise supplies of food for the famishing residents of the garrets and cellars of London lanes and alleys. The quarters of the Salvation Army in various parts of London are nightly besieged by hosts of the unemployed and the hungry for whom neither shelter nor the means of sustenance can be provided.'

It has been urged that the criticism I have passed on things as they are in England is too pessimistic. I must say, in extenuation, that of optimists I am the most optimistic. But I measure manhood less by political aggregations than by individuals. Society grows, while political machines rack to pieces and become 'scrap'. For the English, so far as manhood and womanhood and health and happiness go, I see a broad and smiling future. But for a great deal of the political machinery, which at present mismanages for them, I see nothing else than the scrap heap.

JACK LONDON

Piedmont, California

THE *chief priests and rulers cry:*

'O Lord and Master, not ours the guilt,
We build but as our fathers built;
Behold thine images how they stand
Sovereign and sole through all our land.

'Our task is hard – with sword and flame,
To hold thine earth forever the same,
And with sharp crooks of steel to keep,
Still as thou leftest them, thy sheep.'

Then Christ sought out an artisan,
A low-browed, stunted, haggard man,
And a motherless girl whose fingers thin
Crushed from her faintly want and sin.

These set he in the midst of them,
And as they drew back their garment hem
For fear of defilement, 'Lo, here,' said he,
'The images you have made of me.'

JAMES RUSSELL LOWELL

CHAPTER ONE

THE DESCENT

'But you can't do it, you know,' friends said, to whom I applied for assistance in the matter of sinking myself down into the East End of London. 'You had better see the police for a guide,' they added, on second thought, painfully endeavouring to adjust themselves to the psychological processes of a madman who had come to them with better credentials than brains.

'But I don't want to see the police,' I protested. 'What I wish to do is to go down into the East End and see things for myself. I wish to know how those people are living there, and why they are living there, and what they are living for. In short, I am going to live there myself.'

'You don't want to *live* down there,' everybody said, with disapprobation writ large upon their faces. 'Why, it is said there are places where a man's life isn't worth tu'pence.'

'The very places I wish to see,' I broke in.

'But you can't, you know,' was the unfailing rejoinder.

'Which is not what I came to see you about,' I answered brusquely, somewhat nettled by their incomprehension. 'I am a stranger here, and I want to tell me what you know of the East End, in order that I may have something to start on.'

'But we know nothing of the East End. It is over there, somewhere.' And they waved their hands vaguely in the direction where the sun on rare occasions may be seen to rise.

'Then I shall go to Cook's,' I announced.

'Oh yes,' they said, with relief. 'Cook's will be sure to know.'

But O Cook, O Thomas Cook & Son, pathfinders and trailclearers, living sign-posts to all the world, and bestowers of first aid to bewildered travellers – unhesitatingly and instantly, with ease and celerity, could you send me to Darkest Africa or Innermost Thibet, but to the East End of London, barely a stone's throw distant from Ludgate Circus, you know not the way!

'You can't do it, you know,' said the human emporium of routes and fares at Cook's Cheapside branch. 'It is so – ahem – so unusual.'

'Consult the police,' he concluded authoritatively, when I had persisted. 'We are not accustomed to taking travellers to the East End; we receive no call to take them there, and we know nothing whatsoever about the place at all.'

'Never mind that,' I interposed, to save myself from being swept out of the office by his flood of negations. 'Here's something you can do for me. I wish you to understand in advance what I intend doing, so that in case of trouble you may be able to identify me.'

'Ah, I see! should you be murdered, we would be in position to identify the corpse.'

He said it so cheerfully and cold-bloodedly that on the instant I saw my stark and mutilated cadaver stretched upon a slab where cool waters trickle ceaselessly, and him I saw bending over and sadly and patiently identifying it as the body of the insane American who *would* see the East End.

'No, no,' I answered; 'merely to identify me in case I get into a scrape with the "Bobbies".' This last I said with a thrill; truly, I was gripping hold of the vernacular.

'That,' he said, 'is a matter for the consideration of the Chief Office.

'It is so unprecedented, you know,' he added apologetically.

The man at the Chief Office hemmed and hawed. 'We make it a rule,' he explained, 'to give no information concerning our clients.'

'But in this case,' I urged, 'it is the client who requests you to give the information concerning himself.'

Again he hemmed and hawed.

'Of course,' I hastily anticipated, 'I know it is unprecedented, but—'

'As I was about to remark,' he went on steadily, 'it is unprecedented, and I don't think we can do anything for you.'

However, I departed with the address of a detective who lived in the East End, and took my way to the American consul-general. And here, at last, I found a man with whom I could 'do business'. There was no hemming and hawing, no lifted brows, open incredulity, or blank amazement. In one minute I explained myself and my project, which he accepted as a matter of course. In the second minute he asked my age, height, and weight, and looked me over. And in the third minute, as we shook hands at parting, he said : 'All right, Jack. I'll remember you and keep track.'

I breathed a sigh of relief. Having burnt my ships behind me, I was now free to plunge into that human wilderness of which nobody seemed to know anything. But at once I encountered a new difficulty in the shape of my cabby, a grey-whiskered and eminently decorous personage who had imperturbably driven me for several hours about the 'City'.

'Drive me down to the East End,' I ordered, taking my seat.

'Where, sir?' he demanded with frank surprise.

'To the East End, anywhere. Go on.'

The hansom pursued an aimless way for several minutes, then came to a puzzled stop. The aperture above my head was uncovered, and the cabman peered down perplexedly at me.

'I say,' he said, 'wot plyce yer wanter go?'

'East End,' I repeated. 'Nowhere in particular. Just drive me around anywhere.'

'But wot's the haddress, sir?'

'See here!' I thundered. 'Drive me down to the East End, and at once!'

It was evident that he did not understand, but he withdrew his head, and grumblingly started his horse.

Nowhere in the streets of London may one escape the sight of abject poverty, while five minutes' walk from almost any point will bring one to a slum; but the region my hansom was now penetrating was one unending slum. The streets were filled with a new and different race of people, short of stature, and of wretched or beer-sodden appearance. We rolled along through miles of bricks and squalor, and from each cross street and alley flashed long vistas of bricks and misery. Here and there lurched a drunken man or woman, and the air was obscene with sounds of jangling and squabbling. At a market, tottery old men and women were searching in the garbage thrown in the mud for rotten potatoes, beans, and vegetables, while little children clustered like flies around a festering mass of fruit, thrusting their arms to the shoulders into the liquid corruption, and drawing forth morsels but partially decayed, which they devoured on the spot.

Not a hansom did I meet with in all my drive, while mine was like an apparition from another and better world, the way the children ran after it and alongside. And as far as I could see were the solid walls of brick, the slimy pavements, and the screaming streets; and for the first time in my life the fear of the crowd smote me. It was like the fear of the sea; and the miserable multitudes, street upon street, seemed so many waves of a vast and malodorous sea, lapping about me and threatening to well up and over me.

'Stepney, sir; Stepney Station,' the cabby called down.

I looked about. It was really a railroad station, and he had driven desperately to it as the one familiar spot he had ever heard of in all that wilderness.

'Well,' I said.

He spluttered unintelligibly, shook his head, and looked very miserable. 'I'm a strynger 'ere,' he managed to articulate. 'An' if yer don't want Stepney Station, I'm blessed if I know wotcher do want.'

'I'll tell you what I want,' I said. 'You drive along and keep your eye out for a shop where old clothes are sold. Now, when you see such a shop, drive right on till you turn the corner, then stop and let me out.'

I could see that he was growing dubious of his fare, but not long afterwards he pulled up to the curb and informed me that an old-clothes shop was to be found a bit of the way back.

'Won'tcher py me?' he pleaded. 'There's seven an' six owin' me.'

'Yes,' I laughed, 'and it would be the last I'd see of you.'

'Lord lumme, but it'll be the last I see of you if yer don't py me,' he retorted.

But a crowd of ragged onlookers had already gathered around the cab, and I laughed again and walked back to the old-clothes shop.

Here the chief difficulty was in making the shopman understand that I really and truly wanted old clothes. But after fruitless attempts to press upon me new and impossible coats and trousers, he began to bring to light heaps of old ones, looking mysterious the while and hinting darkly. This he did with the palpable intention of letting me know that he had 'piped my lay', in order to bulldoze me, through fear of exposure, into paying heavily for my purchases. A

13

man in trouble, or a high-class criminal from across the water, was what he took my measure for – in either case, a person anxious to avoid the police.

But I disputed with him over the outrageous difference between prices and values, till I quite disabused him of the notion, and he settled down to drive a hard bargain with a hard customer. In the end I selected a pair of stout though well-worn trousers, a frayed jacket with one remaining button, a pair of brogans which had plainly seen service where coal was shovelled, a thin leather belt, and a very dirty cloth cap. My underclothing and socks, however, were new and warm, but of the sort that any American waif, down in his luck, could acquire in the ordinary course of events.

'I must sy yer a sharp 'un,' he said, with counterfeit admiration, as I handed over the ten shillings finally agreed upon for the outfit. 'Blimey, if you ain't ben up an' down Petticut Lane afore now. Yer trouseys is wuth five bob to hany man, an' a docker 'ud give two an' six for the shoes, to sy nothin' of the coat an' cap an' new stoker's singlet an' hother things.'

'How much will you give me for them?' I demanded suddenly. 'I paid you ten bob for the lot, and I'll sell them back to you, right now, for eight. Come, it's a go!'

But he grinned and shook his head, and though I had made a good bargain, I was unpleasantly aware that he had made a better one.

I found the cabby and a policeman with their heads together, but the latter, after looking me over sharply, and particularly scrutinizing the bundle under my arm, turned away and left the cabby to wax mutinous by himself. And not a step would he budge till I paid him the seven shillings and sixpence owing him. Whereupon he was willing to drive me to the ends of the earth, apologizing profusely for his insistence, and explaining that one ran across queer customers in London Town.

But he drove me only to Highbury Vale, in North London, where my luggage was waiting for me. Here, next day, I took off my shoes (not without regret for their lightness and comfort), and my soft, grey travelling suit, and, in fact, all my clothing; and proceeded to array myself in the clothes of the other and unimaginable men, who must have been indeed unfortunate to have had to part with such rags for the pitiable sums obtainable from a dealer.

Inside my stoker's singlet, in the armpit, I sewed a gold sovereign (an emergency sum certainly of modest proportions); and inside my stoker's singlet I put myself. And then I sat down and moralized upon the fair years and fat, which had made my skin soft and brought the nerves close to the surface; for the singlet was rough and raspy as a hair shirt, and I am confident that the most rigorous of ascetics suffer no more than I did in the ensuing twenty-four hours.

The remainder of my costume was fairly easy to put on, though the brogans, or brogues, were quite a problem. As stiff and hard as if made of wood, it was only after a prolonged pounding of the uppers with my fists that I was able to get my feet into them at all. Then, with a few shillings, a knife, a handkerchief, and some brown papers and flake tobacco stowed away in my pockets, I thumped down the stairs and said good-bye to my foreboding friends. As I passed out of the door, the 'help', a comely middle-aged woman, could not conquer a grin that twisted her lips and separated them till the throat, out of involuntary sympathy, made the uncouth animal noises we are wont to designate as 'laughter'.

No sooner was I out on the streets than I was impressed by the difference in status effected by my clothes. All servility vanished from the demeanour of the common people with whom I came in contact. Presto! In the twinkling of an eye, so to say, I had become one of them. My frayed and out-at-elbows jacket was the badge and advertisement of my class, which was their class. It made me of like kind, and in place of the fawning and too respectful attention I had hitherto received, I now shared with them a comradeship. The man in corduroy and dirty neckerchief no longer addressed me as 'sir' or 'governor'. It was 'mate' now – and a fine and hearty word, with a tingle to it, and a warmth and gladness, which the other term does not possess. Governor! It smacks of mastery, and power, and high authority – the tribute of the man who is under to the man on top, delivered in the hope that he will let up a bit and ease his weight, which is another way of saying that it is an appeal for alms.

This brings me to a delight I experienced in my rags and tatters which is denied the average American abroad. The European traveller from the States, who is not a Croesus, speedily finds himself reduced to a chronic state of self-conscious sordidness by the hordes of cringing robbers who clutter his steps from dawn till dark, and deplete his pocket-book in a way that puts compound interest to the blush.

In my rags and tatters I escaped the pestilence of tipping, and encountered men on a basis of equality. Nay, before the day was out I turned the tables, and said, most gratefully, 'Thank you, sir,' to a gentleman whose horse I held, and who dropped a penny into my eager palm.

Other changes I discovered were wrought in my condition by my new garb. In crossing crowded thoroughfares I found I had to be, if anything, more lively in avoiding vehicles, and it was strikingly impressed upon me that my life had cheapened in direct ratio with my clothes. When before I inquired the way of a policeman, I was usually asked, 'Bus or 'ansome, sir?' But now the query became, 'Walk or ride?' Also, at the railway stations, a third-class ticket was now shoved out to me as a matter of course.

But there was compensation for it all. For the first time I met the English lower classes face to face, and knew them for what they were. When loungers and workmen, at street corners and in public-houses, talked with me, they talked as one man to another, and they talked as natural men should talk, without the least idea of getting anything out of me for what they talked or the way they talked.

And when at last I made into the East End, I was gratified to find

15

that the fear of the crowd no longer haunted me. I had become a part of it. The vast and malodorous sea had welled up and over me, or I had slipped gently into it, and there was nothing fearsome about it – with the one exception of the stoker's singlet.

CHAPTER TWO

JOHNNY UPRIGHT

I SHALL not give you the address of Johnny Upright. Let it suffice that he lives in the most respectable street in the East End – a street that would be considered very mean in America, but a veritable oasis in the desert of East London. It is surrounded on every side by close-packed squalor and streets jammed by a young and vile and dirty generation; but its own pavements are comparatively bare of the children who have no other place to play, while it has an air of desertion, so few are the people that come and go.

Each house in this street, as in all the streets, is shoulder to shoulder with its neighbours. To each house there is but one entrance, the front door; and each house is about eighteen feet wide, with a bit of brick-walled yard behind, where, when it is not raining, one may look at a slate-coloured sky. But it must be understood that this is East End opulence we are now considering. Some of the people in this street are even so well-to-do as to keep a 'slavey'. Johnny Upright keeps one, as I well know, she being my first acquaintance in this particular portion of the world.

To Johnny Upright's house I came, and to the door came the 'slavey'. Now, mark you, her position in life was pitiable and contemptible, but it was with pity and contempt that she looked at me. She evinced a plain desire that our conversation should be short. It was Sunday, and Johnny Upright was not at home, and that was all there was to it. But I lingered, discussing whether or not it was all there was to it, till Mrs. Johnny Upright was attracted to the door, where she scolded the girl for not having closed it before turning her attention to me.

No, Mr. Johnny Upright was not at home, and further he saw nobody on Sunday. It is too bad, said I. Was I looking for work? No, quite the contrary; in fact, I had come to see Johnny Upright on business which might be profitable to him.

A change came over the face of things at once. The gentleman in question was at church, but would be home in an hour or thereabouts, when no doubt he could be seen.

Would I kindly step in? – no, the lady did not ask me, though I fished for an invitation by stating that I would go down to the corner and wait in a public-house. And down to the corner I went, but, it being church time, the 'pub' was closed. A miserable drizzle was falling, and, in lieu of better, I took a seat on a neighbourly doorstep and waited.

And here to the doorstep came the 'slavey', very frowzy and very perplexed, to tell me that the missus would let me come back and wait in the kitchen.

'So many people come 'ere lookin' for work,' Mrs. Johnny Upright apologetically explained. 'So I 'ope you won't feel bad the way I spoke.'

'Not at all, not at all,' I replied in my grandest manner, for the nonce investing my rags with dignity. 'I quite understand, I assure you. I suppose people looking for work almost worry you to death?'

'That they do,' she answered, with an eloquent and expressive glance; and thereupon ushered me into, not the kitchen, but the dining-room – a favour, I took it, in recompense for my grand manner.

This dining-room, on the same floor as the kitchen, was about four feet below the level of the ground, and so dark (it was midday) that I had to wait a space for my eyes to adjust themselves to the gloom. Dirty light filtered in through a window, the top of which was on a level with a sidewalk, and in this light I found that I was able to read newspaper print.

And here, while waiting the coming of Johnny Upright, let me explain my errand. While living, eating, and sleeping with the people of the East End, it was my intention to have a port of refuge, not too far distant, into which I could run now and again to assure myself that good clothes and cleanliness still existed. Also in such port I could receive my mail, work up my notes, and sally forth occasionally in changed garb to civilization.

But this involved a dilemma. A lodging where my property would be safe implied a landlady apt to be suspicious of a gentleman leading a double life; while a landlady who would not bother her head over the double life of her lodgers would imply lodgings where property was unsafe. To avoid the dilemma was what had brought me to Johnny Upright. A detective of thirty-odd years' continuous service in the East End, known far and wide by a name given him by a convicted felon in the dock, he was just the man to find me an honest landlady, and make her rest easy concerning the strange comings and goings of which I might be guilty.

His two daughters beat him home from church – and pretty girls they were in their Sunday dresses; withal it was the certain weak and delicate prettiness which characterizes the Cockney lasses, a prettiness which is no more than a promise with no grip on time, and doomed to fade quickly away like the colour from a sunset sky.

They looked me over with frank curiosity, as though I were some sort of a strange animal, and then ignored me utterly for the rest of my wait. Then Johnny Upright himself arrived, and I was summoned upstairs to confer with him.

'Speak loud,' he interrupted my opening words. 'I've got a bad cold, and I can't hear well.'

Shades of Old Sleuth and Sherlock Holmes! I wondered as to where the assistant was located whose duty it was to take down whatever information I might loudly vouchsafe. And to this day, much as I have seen of Johnny Upright and much as I have puzzled

17

over the incident, I have never been quite able to make up my mind as to whether or not he had a cold, or had an assistant planted in the other room. But of one thing I am sure: though I gave Johnny Upright the facts concerning myself and project, he withheld judgment till next day, when I dodged into his street conventionally garbed and in a hansom. Then his greeting was cordial enough, and I went down into the dining-room to join the family at tea.

'We are humble here,' he said, 'not given to the flesh, and you must take us for what we are, in our humble way.'

The girls were flushed and embarrassed at greeting me, while he did not make it any the easier for them.

'Ha! ha!' he roared heartily, slapping the table with his open hand till the dishes rang. 'The girls thought yesterday you had come to ask for a piece of bread! Ha! ha! ho! ho! ho!'

This they indignantly denied, with snapping eyes and guilty red cheeks, as though it were an essential of true refinement to be able to discern under his rag a man who had no need to go ragged.

And then, while I ate bread and marmalade, proceeded a play at cross purposes, the daughters deeming it an insult to me that I should have been mistaken for a beggar, and the father considering it as the highest compliment to my cleverness to succeed in being so mistaken. All of which I enjoyed, and the bread, and the marmalade, and the tea, till the time came for Johnny Upright to find me a lodging, which he did, not half-a-dozen doors away, in his own respectable and opulent street, in a house as like to his own as a pea to its mate.

CHAPTER THREE

MY LODGING AND SOME OTHERS

FROM an East London standpoint, the room I rented for six shillings, or a dollar and a half, per week, was a most comfortable affair. From the American standpoint, on the other hand, it was rudely furnished, uncomfortable, and small. By the time I had added an ordinary typewriter table to its scanty furnishing, I was hard put to turn around; at the best, I managed to navigate it by a sort of vermicular progression requiring great dexterity and presence of mind.

Having settled myself, or my property rather, I put on my knockabout clothes and went out for a walk. Lodgings being fresh in my mind, I began to look them up, bearing in mind the hypothesis that I was a poor young man with a wife and large family.

My first discovery was that empty houses were few and far between – so far between, in fact, that though I walked miles in irregular circles over a large area, I still remained between. Not one empty house could I find – a conclusive proof that the district was 'saturated'.

It being plain that as a poor young man with a family I could rent no houses at all in this most undesirable region, I next looked

IN WAPPING

A SMALL DOSS HOUSE

for rooms, unfurnished rooms, in which I could store my wife and babies and chattels. There were not many, but I found them, usually in the singular, for one appears to be considered sufficient for a poor man's family in which to cook and eat and sleep. When I asked for two rooms, the sublettees looked at me very much in the manner, I imagine, that a certain personage looked at Oliver Twist when he asked for more.

Not only was one room deemed sufficient for a poor man and his family, but I learned that many families, occupying single rooms, had so much space to spare as to be able to take in a lodger or two. When such rooms can be rented for from three to six shillings per week, it is a fair conclusion that a lodger with references should obtain floor space for, say, from eightpence to a shilling. He may even be able to board with the sublettees for a few shillings more. This, however, I failed to inquire into – a reprehensible error on my part, considering that I was working on the basis of a hypothetical family.

Not only did the houses I investigated have no bath-tubs, but I learned that there were no bath-tubs in all the thousands of houses I had seen. Under the circumstances with my wife and babies and a couple of lodgers suffering from the too great spaciousness of one room, taking a bath in a tin wash-basin would be an unfeasible undertaking. But, it seems, the compensation comes in with the saving of soap, so all's well, and God's still in heaven.

However, I rented no rooms, but returned to my own Johnny Upright's street. What with my wife, and babies, and lodgers, and the various cubby-holes into which I had fitted them, my mind's eye had become narrow-angled, and I could not quite take in all of my own room at once. The immensity of it was awe-inspiring. Could this be the room I had rented for six shillings a week? Impossible! But my landlady, knocking at the door to learn if I were comfortable, dispelled my doubts.

'Oh yes, sir,' she said, in reply to a question. 'This street is the very last. All the other streets were like this eight or ten years ago, and all the people were very respectable. But the others have driven our kind out. Those in this street are the only ones left. It's shocking, sir!'

And then she explained the process of saturation, by which the rental value of a neighbourhood went up, while its tone went down.

'You see, sir, our kind are not used to crowding in the way the others do. We need more room. The others, the foreigners and lower-class people, can get five and six families into this house, where we only get one. So they can pay more rent for the house than we can afford. It *is* shocking, sir; and just to think, only a few years ago all this neighbourhood was just as nice as it could be.'

I looked at her. Here was a woman, of the finest grade of the English working-class, with numerous evidences of refinement, being slowly engulfed by that noisome and rotten tide of humanity which the powers that be are pouring eastward out of London Town. Bank, factory, hotel, and office building must go up, and the city poor folk are a nomadic breed; so they migrate eastward, wave upon wave, saturating and degrading neighbourhood by neighbour-hood, driving the better class of workers before them to pioneer on the rim of the city, or dragging them down, if not in the first generation, surely in the second and third.

It is only a question of months when Johnny Upright's street must go. He realizes it himself.

'In a couple of years,' he says, 'my lease expires. My landlord is one of our kind. He has not put up the rent on any of his houses here, and this has enabled us to stay. But any day he may sell, or any day he may die, which is the same thing so far as we are concerned. The house is bought by a money breeder, who builds a sweat shop on the patch of ground at the rear where my grapevine is, adds to the house, and rents a room to a family. There you are, and Johnny Upright's gone!'

And truly I saw Johnny Upright, and his good wife and fair daughters, and frowzy slavey, like so many ghosts flitting eastward through the gloom, the monster city roaring at their heels.

But Johnny Upright is not alone in his flitting. Far, far out, on the fringe of the city, live the small business men, little managers, and successful clerks. They dwell in cottages and semi-detached villas, with bits of flower garden, and elbow room, and breathing space. They inflate themselves with pride, and throw out their chests when they contemplate the Abyss from which they have escaped, and they thank God that they are not as other men. And lo! down upon them comes Johnny Upright and the monster city at his heels. Tenements spring up like magic, gardens are built upon, villas are divided and sub-divided into many dwellings, and the black night of London settles down in a greasy pall.

CHAPTER FOUR

A MAN AND THE ABYSS

'I say, can you let a lodging?'

These words I discharged carelessly over my shoulder at a stout and elderly woman, of whose fare I was partaking in a greasy coffee-house down near the Pool and not very far from Limehouse.

'Oh yus,' she answered shortly, my appearance possibly not approximating the standard of affluence required by her house.

I said no more, consuming my rasher of bacon and pint of sickly tea in silence. Nor did she take further interest in me till I came to pay my reckoning (fourpence), when I pulled all of ten shillings out of my pocket. The expected result was produced.

'Yus, sir,' she at once volunteered; 'I 'ave nice lodgin's you'd likely tyke a fancy to. Back from a voyage, sir?'

'How much for a room?' I inquired, ignoring her curiosity.

She looked me up and down with frank surprise. 'I don't let rooms, not to my reg'lar lodgers, much less casuals.'

'Then I'll have to look along a bit,' I said, with marked disappointment.

But the sight of my ten shillings had made her keen. 'I can let you have a nice bed in with two hother men,' she urged. 'Good, respectable men, an' steady.'

'But I don't want to sleep with two other men,' I objected.

'You don't 'ave to. There's three beds in the room, an' hit's not a very small room.'

'How much?' I demanded.

'Arf a crown a week, two an' six, to a regular lodger. You'll fancy the men, I'm sure. One works in the ware'ouse, an' 'e's been with me two years now. An' the hother's bin with me six – six years, sir, and two months comin' nex' Saturday. 'E's a scene-shifter,' she went on. 'A steady, respectable man, never missin' a night's work in the time 'e's bin with me. An' 'e likes the 'ouse; 'e says as it's the best 'e can do in the w'y of lodgin's. I board 'im, an' the hother lodgers too.'

'I suppose he's saving money right along,' I insinuated innocently.

'Bless you, no! Nor can 'e do as well helsewhere with 'is money.'

And I thought of my own spacious West, with room under its sky and unlimited air for a thousand Londons; and here was this man, a steady and reliable man, never missing a night's work, frugal and honest, lodging in one room with two other men, paying two dollars and a half per month for it, and out of his experience adjudging it to be the best he could do! And here was I, on the strength of the ten shillings in my pocket, able to enter in with my rags and take up my bed with him. The human soul is a lonely thing, but it must be very lonely sometimes when there are three beds to a room, and casuals with ten shillings are admitted.

'How long have you been here?' I asked.

'Thirteen years, sir; an' don't you think you'll fancy the lodgin'?'

The while she talked she was shuffling ponderously about the small kitchen in which she cooked the food for her lodgers who were also boarders. When I first entered, she had been hard at work, nor had she let up once throughout the conversation. Undoubtedly she was a busy woman. 'Up at half-past five,' 'to bed the last thing at night,' 'workin' fit ter drop,' thirteen years of it, and for reward, grey hairs, frowzy clothes, stooped shoulders, slatternly figure, unending toil in a foul and noisome coffee-house that faced on an alley ten feet between the walls, and a waterside environment that was ugly and sickening, to say the least.

'You'll be hin hagain to 'ave a look?' she questioned wistfully, as I went out of the door.

And as I turned and looked at her, I realized to the full the deeper truth underlying that very wise old maxim: 'Virtue is its own reward.'

I went back to her. 'Have you ever taken a vacation?' I asked.

'Vycytion?'

'A trip to the country for a couple of days, fresh air, a day off, you know, a rest.'

21

'Lor' lumme!' she laughed, for the first time stopping from her work. 'A vycytion, eh? for the likes o' me? Just fancy now! – Mind yer feet!' – this last sharply, and to me, as I stumbled over the rotten threshold.

Down near the West India Dock I came upon a young fellow staring disconsolately at the muddy water. A fireman's cap was pulled down across his eyes, and the fit and sag of his clothes whispered unmistakably of the sea.

'Hello, mate,' I greeted him, sparring for a beginning. 'Can you tell me the way to Wapping?'

'Worked yer way over on a cattle boat?' he countered, fixing my nationality on the instant.

And thereupon we entered upon a talk that extended itself to a public-house and a couple of pints of 'arf an' arf'. This led to closer intimacy, so that when I brought to light all of a shilling's worth of coppers (ostensibly my all), and put aside sixpence for a bed, and sixpence for more arf an' arf, he generously proposed that we drink up the whole shilling.

'My mate, 'e cut up rough las' night,' he explained. 'An' the bobbies got 'm, so you can bunk in wi' me. Wotcher say?'

I said yes, and by the time we had soaked ourselves in a whole shilling's worth of beer, and slept the night on a miserable bed in a miserable den, I knew him pretty fairly for what he was. And that in one respect he was representative of a large body of the lower-class London workman, my later experience substantiates.

He was London-born, his father a fireman and a drinker before him. As a child, his home was the streets and the docks. He had never learned to read, and had never felt the need for it – a vain and useless accomplishment, he held, at least for a man of his station in life.

He had had a mother and numerous squalling brothers and sisters, all crammed into a couple of rooms and living on poorer and less regular food than he could ordinarily rustle for himself. In fact, he never went home except at periods when he was unfortunate in procuring his own food. Petty pilfering and begging along the streets and docks, a trip or two to sea as mess-boy, a few trips more as coal-trimmer, and then a full-fledged fireman, he had reached the top of his life.

And in the course of this he had also hammered out a philosophy of life, an ugly and repulsive philosophy, but withal a very logical and sensible one from his point of view. When I asked him what he lived for, he immediately answered, 'Booze.' A voyage to sea (for a man must live and get the wherewithal), and then the paying off and the big drunk at the end. After that, haphazard little drunks, sponged in the 'pubs' from mates with a few coppers left, like myself, and when sponging was played out another trip to sea and a repetition of the beastly cycle.

'But women,' I suggested, when he had finished proclaiming booze the sole end of existence.

'Wimmen!' He thumped his pot upon the bar and orated eloquently. 'Wimmen is a thing my edication 'as learnt me t'let alone.

It don't pay, matey; it don't pay. Wot's a man like me want o' wimmen, eh? jest you tell me. There was my mar, she was enough, a-bangin' the kids about an' r'kin' the ole man mis'rable when 'e come 'ome, w'ich was seldom, I grant. An' fer w'y? Becos o' mar! She didn't make 'is 'ome 'appy, that was w'y. Then, there's the other wimmen, 'ow do they treat a pore stoker with a few shillin's in 'is trouseys? A good drunk is wot 'e's got in 'is pockits, a good long drunk, an' the wimmen skin 'im out of his money so quick 'e ain't 'ad 'ardly a glass. I know. I've 'ad my fling, an I know wot's wot. An' I tell you, where's wimmen is trouble – screechin' an' carryin' on, fightin', cuttin', bobbies, magistrates, an' a month's 'ard labour back of it all, an' no pay-day when you come out.'

'But a wife and children,' I insisted. 'A home of your own, and all that. Think of it, back from a voyage, little children climbing on your knee, and the wife happy and smiling, and a kiss for you when she lays the table, and a kiss all round from the babies when they go to bed, and the kettle singing and the long talk afterwards of where you've been and what you've seen, and of her and all the little happenings at home while you've been away and—'

'Garn!' he cried, with a playful shove of his fist on my shoulder. 'Wot's yer game, eh? A missus kissin' an' kids clim'in', an' kettle singin', all on four poun' ten a month w'en you 'ave a ship, an' four nothin' w'en you 'aven't. I'll tell you wot I'd get on four poun' ten – a missus rowin', kids squallin', no coal t' make the kettle sing, and the kettle up the spout, that's wot I'd get. Enough t' make a bloke bloomin' well glad to be back t' sea. A missus! Wot for? T' make you mis'rable? Kids? Jest take my counsel, matey, an' don't 'ave 'em. Look at me! I can 'ave my beer w'en I like, an' no blessed missus an' kids a-crying for bread. I'm 'appy, I am, with my beer an' mates like you, an' a good ship comin', an' another trip to sea. So I say, let's 'ave another pint. Arf an' arf's good enough for me.'

Without going further with the speech of this young fellow of two-and-twenty, I think I have sufficiently indicated his philosophy of life and the underlying economic reason for it. Home life he had never known. The word 'home' aroused nothing but unpleasant associations. In the low wages of his father, and of other men in the same walk of life, he found sufficient reason for branding wife and children as encumbrances and causes of masculine misery. An unconscious hedonist, utterly unmoral and materialistic, he sought the greatest possible happiness for himself, and found it in drink.

A young sot; a premature wreck; physical inability to do a stoker's work; the butter or the workhouse; and the end – he saw it all as clearly as I, but it held no terrors for him. From the moment of his birth, all the forces of his environment had tended to harden him, and he viewed his wretched, inevitable future with a callousness and unconcern I could not shake.

And yet he was not a bad man. He was not inherently vicious and brutal. He had normal mentality, and a more than average physique. His eyes were blue and round, shaded by long lashes, and wide apart. And there was a laugh in them, and a fund of humour behind. The

23

brow and general features were good, the mouth and lips sweet, though already developing a harsh twist. The chin was weak, but not too weak; I have seen men sitting in the high places with weaker.

His head was shapely, and so gracefully was it poised upon a perfect neck that I was not surprised by his body that night when he stripped for bed. I have seen many men strip, in gymnasium and training quarters, men of good blood and upbringing, but I have never seen one who stripped to better advantage than this young sot of two-and-twenty, this young god doomed to rack and ruin in four or five short years, and to pass hence without posterity to receive the splendid heritage it was his to bequeath.

It seemed sacrilege to waste such life, and yet I was forced to confess that he was right in not marrying on four pounds ten in London Town. Just as the scene-shifter was happier in making both ends meet in a room shared with two other men, than he would have been had he packed a feeble family along with a couple of men into a cheaper room, and failed in making both ends meet.

And day by day I became convinced that not only is it unwise, but it is criminal for the people of the Abyss to marry. They are the stones by the builder rejected. There is no place for them in the social fabric, while all the forces of society drive them downward till they perish. At the bottom of the Abyss they are feeble, besotted, and imbecile. If they reproduce, the life is so cheap that perforce it perishes of itself. The work of the world goes on above them, and they do not care to take part in it, nor are they able. Moreover, the work of the world does not need them. There are plenty, far fitter than they, clinging to the steep slope above, and struggling frantically to slide no more.

In short, the London Abyss is a vast shambles. Year by year, and decade after decade, rural England pours in a flood of vigorous strong life, that not only does not renew itself, but perishes by the third generation. Competent authorities aver that the London workman whose parents and grand-parents were born in London is so remarkable a specimen that he is rarely found.

Mr. A. C. Pigou has said that the aged poor, and the residuum which compose the 'submerged tenth', constitute $7\frac{1}{2}$ per cent of the population of London. Which is to say that last year, and yesterday, and today, at this very moment, 450,000 of these creatures are dying miserably at the bottom of the social pit called 'London'. As to how they die, I shall take an instance from this morning's paper.

SELF-NEGLECT

Yesterday Dr. Wynn Westcott held an inquest at Shoreditch, respecting the death of Elizabeth Crews, aged 77 years, of 32 East Street, Holborn, who died on Wednesday last. Alice Mathieson stated that she was landlady of the house where deceased lived. Witness last saw her alive on the previous Monday. She lived quite alone. Mr. Francis Birch, relieving officer for the Holborn district, stated that deceased had occupied the room in question for thirty-five years. When witness was called, on the 1st, he found the old woman in a terrible state, and the ambulance and coachman had to be disinfected after the removal. Dr. Chase Fennell said death was due to blood-poisoning from bed-sores, due to self-neglect and filthy surroundings, and the jury returned a verdict to that effect.

The most startling thing about this little incident of a woman's death is the smug complacency with which the officials looked upon it and rendered judgment. That an old woman of seventy-seven years of age should die of SELF-NEGLECT is the most optimistic way possible of looking at it. It was the old dead woman's fault that she died, and having located the responsibility, society goes contentedly on about its own affairs.

Of the 'submerged tenth' Mr. Pigou has said: 'Either through lack of bodily strength, or of intelligence, or of fibre, or of all three, they are inefficient or unwilling workers, and consequently unable to support themselves. ... They are often so degraded in intellect as to be incapable of distinguishing their right from their left hand, or of recognizing the numbers of their own houses; their bodies are feeble and without stamina, their affections are warped, and they scarcely know what family life means.'

Four hundred and fifty thousand is a whole lot of people. The young fireman was only one, and it took him some time to say his little say. I should not like to hear them all talk at once. I wonder if God hears them?

CHAPTER FIVE

THOSE ON THE EDGE

My first impression of East London was naturally a general one. Later the details began to appear, and here and there in the chaos of misery I found little spots where a fair measure of happiness reigned – sometimes whole rows of houses in little out-of-the-way streets, where artisans dwell and where a rude sort of family life obtains. In the evenings the men can be seen at the doors, pipes in their mouths and children on their knees, wives gossiping, and laughter and fun going on. The content of these people is manifestly great, for, relative to the wretchedness that encompasses them, they are well off.

But at the best, it is a dull, animal happiness, the content of the full belly. The dominant note of their lives is materialistic. They are stupid and heavy, without imagination. The Abyss seems to exude a stupefying atmosphere of torpor, which wraps about them and deadens them. Religion passes them by. The Unseen holds for them neither terror nor delight. They are unaware of the Unseen; and the full belly and the evening pipe, with their regular 'arf an' arf', is all they demand, or dream of demanding, from existence.

This would not be so bad if it were all; but it is not all. The satisfied torpor in which they are sunk is the deadly inertia that precedes dissolution. There is no progress, and with them not to progress is to fall back and into the Abyss. In their own lives they may only start to fall, leaving the fall to be completed by their children and their children's children. Man always gets less than he demands from life; and so little do they demand, that the less than little they get cannot save them.

At the best, city life is an unnatural life for the human; but the city life of London is so utterly unnatural that the average workman or workwoman cannot stand it. Mind and body are sapped by the undermining influences ceaselessly at work. Moral and physical stamina are broken, and the good workman, fresh from the soil, becomes in the first city generation a poor workman; and by the second city generation, devoid of push and go and initiative, and actually unable physically to perform the labour his father did, he is well on the way to the shambles at the bottom of the Abyss.

If nothing else, the air he breathes, and from which he never escapes, is sufficient to weaken him mentally and physically, so that he becomes unable to compete with the fresh virile life from the country hastening on to London Town to destroy and be destroyed.

Leaving out the disease germs that fills the air of the East End, consider but the one item of smoke. Sir William Thiselton-Dyer, curator of Kew Gardens, has been studying smoke deposits on vegetation, and, according to his calculations, no less than six tons of solid matter, consisting of soot and tarry hydrocarbons, are deposited every week on every quarter of a square mile in and about London. This is equivalent to twenty-four tons per week to the square mile, of 1,248 tons per year to the square mile. From the cornice below the dome of St. Paul's Cathedral was recently taken a solid deposit of crystallized sulphate of lime. This deposit had been formed by the action of the sulphuric acid in the atmosphere upon the carbonate of lime in the stone. And this sulphuric acid in the atmosphere is constantly being breathed by the London workmen through all the days and nights of their lives.

It is incontrovertible that the children grow up into rotten adults, without virility or stamina, a weak-kneed, narrow-chested, listless breed, that crumples up and goes down in the brute struggle for life with the invading hordes from the country. The railway men, carriers, omnibus drivers, corn and timber porters, and all those who require physical stamina, are largely drawn from the country; while in the Metropolitan Police there are, roughly, 12,000 country-born as against 3,000 London-born.

So one is forced to conclude that the Abyss is literally a huge man-killing machine, and when I pass along the little out-of-the-way streets with the full-bellied artisans at the doors, I am aware of a greater sorrow for them than for the 450,000 lost and hopeless wretches dying at the bottom of the pit. They, at least, are dying, that is the point; while these have yet to go through the slow and preliminary pangs extending through two and even three generations.

And yet the quality of the life is good. All human potentialities are in it. Given proper conditions, it could live through the centuries, and great men, heroes and masters, spring from it and make the world better by having lived.

I talked with a woman who was representative of that type which had been jerked out of its little out-of-the-way streets and has started on the fatal fall to the bottom. Her husband was a fitter and a member of the Engineers' Union. That he was a poor engineer was evidenced by his inability to get regular employment. He did not have the energy and enterprise necessary to obtain or hold a steady position.

The pair had two daughters, and the four of them lived in a couple of holes, called 'rooms' by courtesy, for which they paid seven shillings per week. The possessed no stove, managing their cooking on a single gas-ring in the fire-place. Not being persons of property, they were unable to obtain an unlimited supply of gas; but a clever machine had been installed for their benefit. By dropping a penny in the slot, the gas was forthcoming, and when a penny's worth had forthcome the supply was automatically shut off. 'A penny gawn in no time,' she explained, 'an' the cookin' not arf done!'

Incipient starvation had been their portion for years. Month in and month out, they had arisen from the table able and willing to eat more. And when once on the downward slope, chronic innutrition is an important factor in sapping vitality and hastening the descent.

Yet this woman was a hard worker. From 4.30 in the morning till the last light at night, she said, she had toiled at making cloth dress-skirts, lined up and with two flounces, for seven shillings a dozen. Cloth dress-skirts, mark you, lined up with two flounces, for seven shillings a dozen! This is equal to $1.75 per dozen, or 14¾ cents per skirt.

The husband, in order to obtain employment, had to belong to the union, which collected one shilling and sixpence from him each week. Also, when strikes were afoot and he chanced to be working, he had at times been compelled to pay as high as seventeen shillings into the union's coffers for the relief fund.

One daughter, the elder, had worked as green hand for a dress-maker, for one shilling and sixpence a week – 37½ cents per week, or a fraction over 5 cents per day. However, when the slack season came she was discharged, though she had been taken on at such low pay with the understanding that she was to learn the trade and work up. After that she had been employed in a bicycle store for three years, for which she received five shillings per week, walking two miles to her work, and two back, and being fined for tardiness.

As far as the man and woman were concerned, the game was played. They had lost handhold and foothold, and were falling into the pit. But what of the daughters? Living like swine, enfeebled by chronic innutrition, being sapped mentally, morally, and physic-ally, what chance have they to crawl up and out of the Abyss into which they were born falling?

As I write this, and for an hour past, the air has been made hideous by a free-for-all, rough-and-tumble fight going on in the yard that is back to back with my yard. When the first sounds reached me I took it for the barking and snarling of dogs, and some minutes were required to convince me that human beings, and women at that, could produce such a fearful clamour.

Drunken women fighting! It is not nice to think of; it is far worse to listen to. Something like this it runs—

Incoherent babble, shrieked at the top of the lungs of several women; a lull, in which is heard a child crying and a young girl's voice pleading tearfully; a woman's voice rises, harsh and grating, 'You 'it me! Jest you 'it me!' then, swat! challenge accepted and fight rages afresh.

The back windows of the houses commanding the scene are lined with enthusiastic spectators, and the sound of blows, and of oaths that make one's blood run cold, are borne to my ears. Happily, I cannot see the combatants.

A lull; 'You let that child alone!' child evidently of few years, screaming in downright terror. 'Awright,' repeated insistently and at top pitch twenty times straight running; 'you'll git this rock on the 'ead!' and then rock evidently on the head from the shriek that goes up.

A lull; apparently one combatant temporarily disabled and being resuscitated; child's voice audible again, but now sunk to a lower note of terror and growing exhaustion.

Voices begin to go up the scale, something like this:

'Yes?'
'Yes!'
'Yes?'
'Yes!'
'Yes?'
'Yes!'
'Yes?'
'Yes!'

Sufficient affirmation on both sides, conflict again precipitated. One combatant gets overwhelming advantage, and follows it up from the way the other combatant screams bloody murder. Bloody murder gurgles and dies out, undoubtedly throttled by a strangle hold.

Entrance of new voices; a flank attack; strangle hold suddenly broken from the way bloody murder goes up half an octave higher than before; general hullaballoo, everybody fighting.

Lull; new voice, young girl's, 'I'm goin' ter tyke my mother's part;' dialogue, repeated about five times, 'I'll do as I like, blankety, blank, blank!' 'I'd like ter see yer, blankety, blank, blank!' renewed conflict, mothers, daughters, everybody, during which my landlady calls her young daughter in from the back steps, while I wonder what will be the effect of all that she has heard upon her moral fibre.

28

CHAPTER SIX

FRYING-PAN ALLEY AND A
GLIMPSE OF INFERNO

THREE of us walked down Mile End Road, and one was a hero. He was a slender lad of nineteen, so slight and frail, in fact, that like Fra Lippo Lippi, a puff of wind might double him up and turn him over. He was a burning young socialist, in the first throes of enthusiasm and ripe for martyrdom. As platform speaker or chairman he had taken an active and dangerous part in the many indoor and outdoor pro-Boer meetings which have vexed the serenity of Merry England these several years back. Little items he had been imparting to me as he walked along; of being mobbed in parks and on tram-cars; of climbing on the platform to lead the forlorn hope, when brother speaker after brother speaker had been dragged down by the angry crowd and cruelly beaten; of a siege in a church, where he and three others had taken sanctuary, and where, amid flying missiles and the crashing of stained glass, they had fought off the mob till rescued by platoons of constables; of pitched and giddy battles on stairways, galleries, and balconies; of smashed windows, collapsed stairways, wrecked lecture halls, and broken heads and bones – and then, with a regretful sigh, he looked at me and said: 'How I envy you big, strong men! I'm such a little mite I can't do much when it comes to fighting.'

And I, walking head and shoulders above my two companions, remembered my own husky West, and the stalwart men it had been my custom, in turn, to envy there. Also, as I looked at the mite of a youth with the heart of a lion, I thought, this is the type that on occasion rears barricades and shows the world that men have not forgotten how to die.

But up spoke my other companion, a man of twenty-eight, who eked out a precarious existence in a sweating den.

'I'm a 'earty man, I am,' he announced. 'Not like the other chaps at my shop, I ain't. They consider me a fine specimen of manhood. W'y, d' ye know, I weigh ten stone!'

I was ashamed to tell him that I weighed one hundred and seventy pounds, or over twelve stone, so I contented myself with taking his measure. Poor, misshapen little man! His skin an unhealthy colour, body gnarled and twisted out of all decency, contracted chest, shoulders bent prodigiously from long hours of toil, and head hanging heavily forward and out of place! A ' 'earty man', 'e was!

'How tall are you?'

'Five foot two,' he answered proudly; 'an' the chaps at the shop ...'

'Let me see that shop,' I said.

The shop was idle just then, but I still desired to see it. Passing

Leman Street, we cut off to the left into Spitalfields, and dived into Frying-pan Alley. A spawn of children cluttered the slimy pavement, for all the world like tadpoles just turned frogs on the bottom of a dry pond. In a narrow doorway, so narrow that perforce we stepped over her, sat a woman with a young babe, nursing at breasts grossly naked and libelling all the sacredness of motherhood. In the black and narrow hall behind her we waded through a mess of young life, and essayed an even narrower and fouler stairway. Up we went, three flights, each landing two feet by three in area, and heaped with filth and refuse.

There were seven rooms in this abomination called a house. In six of the rooms, twenty-odd people, of both sexes and all ages, cooked, ate, slept, and worked. In size the rooms averaged eight feet by eight, or possibly nine. The seventh room we entered. It was the den in which five men 'sweated'. It was seven feet wide by eight long, and the table at which the work was performed took up the major portion of the space. On this table were five lasts, and there was barely room for the men to stand to their work, for the rest of the space was heaped with cardboard, leather, bundles of shoe uppers, and a miscellaneous assortment of materials used in attaching the uppers of shoes to their soles.

In the adjoining room lived a woman and six children. In another vile hole lived a widow, with an only son of sixteen who was dying of consumption. The woman hawked sweetmeats on the street, I was told, and more often failed than not to supply her son with the three quarts of milk he daily required. Further, this son, weak and dying, did not taste meat oftener than once a week; and the kind and quality of this meat cannot possibly be imagined by people who have never watched human swine eat.

'The w'y 'e coughs is somethin' terrible,' volunteered my sweated friend, referring to the dying boy. 'We 'ear 'im 'ere, w'ile we're workin', an it's terrible, I say, terrible!'

And, what of the coughing and sweetmeats, I found another menace added to the hostile environment of the children of the slum.

My sweated friend, when work was to be had, toiled with four other men in his eight-by-seven room. In the winter a lamp burned nearly all the day and added its fumes to the over-loaded air, which was breathed, and breathed, and breathed again.

In good times, when there was a rush of work, this man told me that he could earn as high as 'thirty bob a week.' – Thirty shillings! Seven dollars and a half!

'But it's only the best of us can do it,' he qualified. 'An' then we work twelve, thirteen, and fourteen hours a day, just as fast as we can. An' you should see us sweat! Just running from us! If you could see us, it'd dazzle your eyes – tacks flyin' out of mouth like from a machine. Look at my mouth.'

I looked. The teeth were worn down by the constant friction of the metallic brads, while they were coal-black and rotten.

'I clean my teeth,' he added, 'else they'd be worse.'

After he had told me that the workers had to furnish their own tools, brads, 'grindery', cardboard, rent, light, and what not, it was plain that his thirty bob was a diminishing quantity.

'But how long does the rush season last, in which you receive this high wage of thirty bob?' I asked.

'Four months,' was the answer; and for the rest of the year, he informed me, they average from 'half a quid' to a 'quid' a week, which is equivalent to from two dollars and a half to five dollars. The present week was half gone, and he had earned four bob, or one dollar. And yet I was given to understand that this was one of the better grades of sweating.

I looked out of the window, which should have commanded the back yards of the neighbouring buildings. But there were no back-yards, or, rather, they were covered with one-storey hovels, cow-sheds, in which people lived. The roofs of these hovels were covered with deposits of filth, in some places a couple of feet deep – the contributions from the back windows of the second and third storeys. I could make out fish and meat bones, garbage, pestilential rags, old boots, broken earthenware, and all the general refuse of a human sty.

'This is the last year of this trade; they're getting machines to do away with us,' said the sweated one mournfully, as we stepped over the woman with the breasts grossly naked and waded anew through the cheap young life.

We next visited the municipal dwellings erected by the London County Council on the site of the slums where lived Arthur Morrison's 'Child of the Jago'. While the buildings housed more people than before, it was much healthier. But the dwellings were inhabited by the better-class workmen and artisans. The slum people had simply drifted on to crowd other slums or to form new slums.

'An' now,' said the sweated one, the 'earty man who worked so fast as to dazzle one's eyes, 'I'll show you one of London's lungs. This is Spitalfields Garden.' And he mouthed the word 'garden' with scorn.

The shadow of Christ Church falls across Spitalfields Garden, and in the shadow of Christ's Church, at three o'clock in the afternoon, I saw a sight I never wish to see again. There are no flowers in this garden, which is smaller than my own rose garden at home. Grass only grows here, and it is surrounded by a sharp-spiked iron fencing, as are all the parks of London Town, so that homeless men and women may not come in at night and sleep upon it.

As we entered the garden, an old woman between fifty and sixty, passed us, striding with sturdy intention if somewhat rickety action, with two bulky bundles, covered with sacking, slung fore and aft upon her. She was a woman tramp, a houseless soul, too independent to drag her failing carcase through the workhouse door. Like the snail, she carried her home with her. In the two sacking-covered bundles were her household goods, her wardrobe, linen, and dear feminine possessions.

We went up the narrow gravelled walk. On the benches on either side arrayed a mass of miserable and distorted humanity, the sight of which would have impelled Doré to more diabolical flights of fancy than he ever succeeded in achieving. It was a welter of rags and filth, of all manner of loathsome skin diseases, open sores, bruises, grossness, indecency, leering monstrosities and bestial faces. A chill, raw wind was blowing, and these creatures huddled there in their rags, sleeping for the most part, or trying to sleep. Here were a dozen women, ranging in age from twenty years to seventy. Next a babe, possibly of nine months, lying asleep, flat on the hard bench, with neither pillow nor covering, nor with anyone looking after it. Next half-a-dozen men, sleeping bolt upright or leaning against one another in their sleep. In one place a family group, a child asleep in its sleeping mother's arm, and the husband (or male mate) clumsily mending a dilapidated shoe. On another bench a woman trimming the frayed strips of her rags with a knife, and another woman, with thread and needle, sewing up rents. Adjoining, a man holding a sleeping woman in his arms. Farther on, a man, his clothing caked with gutter mud, asleep, with head in the lap of a woman, not more than twenty-five years old, and also asleep.

It was this sleeping that puzzled me. Why were nine out of ten of them asleep or trying to sleep? But it was not till afterwards that I learned. *It is a law of the powers that be that the homeless shall not sleep by night.* On the pavement, by the portico of Christ's Church, where the stone pillars rise towards the sky in a stately row, were whole rows of men lying asleep or drowsing, and all too deep sunk in torpor to rouse or be made curious by our intrusion.

'A lung of London,' I said; 'nay, an abscess, a great putrescent sore.'

'Oh, why did you bring me here?' demanded the burning young socialist, his delicate face white with sickness of soul and stomach sickness.

'Those women there,' said our guide, 'will sell themselves for thru'pence, or tu'pence, or a loaf of stale bread.'

He said it with a cheerful sneer.

But what more he might have said I do not know, for the sick man cried, 'For heaven's sake let us get out of this.'

CHAPTER SEVEN

A WINNER OF THE VICTORIA CROSS

I HAVE found that it is not easy to get into the casual ward of the workhouse. I have made two attempts now, and I shall shortly make a third. The first time I started out at seven o'clock in the evening with four shillings in my pocket. Herein I committed two errors. In the first place, the applicant for admission to the casual ward must be destitute, and as he is subjected to a rigorous search, he must really be destitute; and fourpence, much less four shillings, is sufficient affluence to disqualify him. In the second place, I made

SPITALFIELDS GARDEN

THE POPLAR WORKHOUSE

in the next paragraph. As I say, we walked along, and when they grew bitter and cursed the land, I cursed with them, cursed as an American waif would curse, stranded in a strange and terrible land. And, as I tried to lead them to believe, and succeeded in making them believe, they took me for a 'seafaring man', who had spent his money in riotous living, lost his clothes (no unusual occurrence with seafaring men ashore), and was temporarily broke while looking for a ship. This accounted for my ignorance of English ways in general and casual wards in particular, and my curiosity concerning the same.

The Carter was hard put to keep the pace at which we walked (he told me that he had eaten nothing that day), but the Carpenter, lean and hungry, his grey and ragged overcoat flapping mournfully in the breeze, swung on in a long and tireless stride which reminded me strongly of the plains wolf or coyote. Both kept their eyes upon the pavement as they walked and talked, and every now and then one or the other would stoop and pick something up, never missing the stride the while. I thought it was cigar and cigarette stumps they were collecting, and for some time took no notice. Then I did notice.

From the slimy, spittle-drenched sidewalk, they were picking up bits of orange peel, apple skin, and grape stems, and they were eating them. The pits of greengage plums they cracked between their teeth for the kernels inside. They picked up stray crumbs of bread the size of peas, apple cores so black and dirty one would not take them to be apple cores, and these things these two men took into their mouths, and chewed them, and swallowed them; and this, between six and seven o'clock in the evening of August 20, year of our Lord 1902, in the heart of the greatest, wealthiest, and most powerful empire the world has ever seen.

These two men talked. They were not fools, they were merely old. And naturally, their guts a-reek with pavement offal, they talked of bloody revolution. They talked as anarchists, fanatics, and madmen would talk. And who shall blame them? In spite of my three good meals that day, and the snug bed I could occupy if I wished, and my social philosophy, and my evolutionary belief in the slow development and metamorphosis of things – in spite of all this, I say, I felt impelled to talk rot with them or hold my tongue. Poor fools! Not of their sort are revolutions bred. And when they are dead and dust, which will be shortly, other fools will talk bloody revolution as they gather offal from the spittle-drenched sidewalks along Mile End Road to Poplar Workhouse.

Being a foreigner, and a young man, the Carter and the Carpenter explained things to me and advised me. Their advice, by the way, was brief and to the point; it was to get out of the country. 'As fast as God'll let me,' I assured them; 'I'll hit only the high places, till you won't be able to see my trail for smoke.' They felt the force of my figures, rather than understood them, and they nodded their heads approvingly.

'Actually make a man a criminal against 'is will,' said the Carpenter. ''Ere I am, old, younger men takin' my place, my clothes

37

gettin' shabbier an' shabbier, an' makin' it 'arder ever day to get a job. I go to the casual ward for a bed. Must be there by two or three in the afternoon or I won't get in. You saw what happened today. What chance does that give me to look for work? S'pose I do get into the casual ward? Keep me in all day tomorrow, let me out mornin' o' next day. What then? The law sez I can't get in another casual ward that night less'n ten miles distant. Have to hurry an' walk to be there in time that day. What chance does that give me to look for a job? S'pose I don't walk. S'pose I look for a job? In no time there's night come, an' no bed. No sleep all night, nothin' to eat, what shape am I in the mornin' to look for work? Got to make up my sleep in the park somehow' (the vision of Christ's Church, Spitalfield, was strong on me) 'an' get something to eat. An' there I am! Old, down, an' no chance to get up.'

'Used to be a toll-gate 'ere,' said the Carter. 'Many's the time I've paid my toll 'ere in my cartin' days.'

'I've 'ad three 'a'penny rolls in two days,' the Carpenter announced, after a long pause in the conversation. 'Two of them I ate yesterday, an' the third today,' he concluded, after another long pause.

'I ain't 'ad anything today,' said the Carter. 'An' I'm fagged out. My legs is hurtin' me something fearful.'

'The roll you get in the "spike" is that 'ard you can't eat it nicely with less'n a pint of water,' said the Carpenter, for my benefit. And, on asking him what the 'spike' was, he answered. 'The casual ward. It's a cant word, you know.'

But what surprised me was that he should have the word 'cant' in his vocabulary, a vocabulary that I found was no mean one before we parted.

I asked them what I might expect in the way of treatment, if we succeeded in getting into the Poplar Workhouse, and between them I was supplied with much information. Having taken a cold bath on entering, I would be given for supper six ounces of bread, and 'three parts of skilly'. 'Three parts' means threequarters of a pint, and 'skilly' is a fluid concoction of three quarts of oatmeal stirred into three buckets and a half of hot water.

'Milk and sugar, I suppose, and a silver spoon?' I queried.

'No fear. Salt's what you'll get, an' I've seen some places where you'd not get any spoon. 'Old 'er up an' let 'er run down, that's 'ow they do it.'

'You do get good skilly at 'Ackney,' said the Carter.

'Oh, wonderful skilly, that,' praised the Carpenter, and each looked eloquently at the other.

'Flour an' water at St. George's in the East,' said the Carter.

The Carpenter nodded. He had tried them all.

'Then what?' I demanded.

And I was informed that I was sent directly to bed. 'Call you at half after five in the mornin', an' you get up an' take a "sluice" – if there's any soap. Then breakfast, same as supper, three parts o' skilly an' a six-ounce loaf.'

38

' 'Tisn't always six ounces,' corrected the Carter.

' 'Tisn't, no; an' often that sour you can 'ardly eat it. When first I started I couldn't eat the skilly nor the bread, but now I can eat my own an' another man's portion.'

'I could eat three other men's portions,' said the Carter. 'I haven't 'ad a bit this blessed day.'

'Then what?'

'Then you've got to do your task, pick four pounds of oakum, or clean an' scrub, or break ten to eleven hundredweight of stones. I don't 'ave to break stones; I'm past sixty, you see. They'll make you do it, though. You're young an' strong.'

'What I don't like,' grumbled the Carter, 'is to be locked up in a cell to pick oakum. It's too much like prison.'

'But suppose, after you've had your night's sleep, you refuse to pick oakum, or break stones, or do any work at all?' I asked.

'No fear you'll refuse the second time; they'll run you in,' answered the Carpenter. 'Wouldn't advise you to try it on, my lad.'

'Then comes dinner,' he went on. 'Eight ounces of bread, one and a arf ounces of cheese, an' cold water. Then you finish your task an' 'ave supper, same as before, three parts o' skilly an' six ounces o' bread. Then to bed, six o'clock, an' next mornin' you're turned loose, provided you've finished your task.'

We had long since left Mile End Road, and after traversing a gloomy maze of narrow, winding streets, we came to Poplar Workhouse. On a low stone wall we spread our handkerchiefs, and each in his handkerchief put all his worldly possessions, with the exception of the 'bit o' baccy' down his sock. And then, as the last light was fading from the drab-coloured sky, the wind blowing cheerless and cold, we stood, with our pitiful little bundles in our hands, a forlorn group at the workhouse door.

Three working girls came along, and one looked pityingly at me; as she passed I followed her with my eyes, and she still looked pityingly back at me. The old men she did not notice. Dear Christ, she pitied me, young and vigorous and strong, but she had no pity for the two old men who stood by my side! She was a young woman, and I was a young man, and what vague sex promptings impelled her to pity me put her sentiment on the lowest plane. Pity for old men is an altruistic feeling, and besides, the workhouse door is the accustomed place for old men. So she showed no pity for them, only for me, who deserved it least or not at all. Not in honour do grey hairs go down to the grave in London Town.

On one side the door was a bell handle, on the other side a press button.

'Ring the bell,' said the Carter to me.

And just as I ordinarily would at anybody's door, I pulled out the handle and rang a peal.

'Oh! Oh!' they cried in one terrified voice. 'Not so 'ard!'

I let go, and they looked reproachfully at me, as though I had imperilled their chance for a bed and three parts of skilly. Nobody came. Luckily, it was the wrong bell, and I felt better.

'Press the button,' I said to the Carpenter.

'No, no, wait a bit,' the Carter hurriedly interposed.

From all of which I drew the conclusion that a poorhouse porter, who commonly draws a yearly salary of from seven to nine pounds, is a very finicky and important personage, and cannot be treated too fastidiously by – paupers.

So we waited, ten times a decent interval, when the Carter stealthily advanced a timid forefinger to the button, and gave it the faintest, shortest possible push. I have looked at waiting men where life or death was in the issue; but anxious suspense showed less plainly on their faces than it showed on the faces of these two men as they waited on the coming of the porter.

He came. He barely looked at us. 'Full up,' he said and shut the door.

'Another night of it,' groaned the Carpenter. In the dim light the Carter looked wan and grey.

Indiscriminate charity is vicious, say the professional philanthropists. Well, I resolved to be vicious.

'Come on; get your knife out and come here,' I said to the Carter, drawing him into a dark alley.

He glared at me in a frightened manner, and tried to draw back. Possibly he took me for a latter-day Jack-the-Ripper, with a penchant for elderly male paupers. Or he may have thought I was inveigling him into the commission of some desperate crime. Anyway, he was frightened.

It will be remembered, at the outset, that I sewed a pound inside my stoker's singlet under the armpit. This was an emergency fund, and I was now called upon to use it for the first time.

Not until I had gone through the acts of a contortionist, and shown the round coin sewed in, did I succeed in getting the Carter's help. Even then his hand was trembling so that I was afraid he would cut me instead of the stitches, and I was forced to take the knife away and do it myself. Out rolled the gold piece, a fortune in their hungry eyes; and away we stampeded for the nearest coffee-house.

Of course I had to explain to them that I was merely an investigator, a social student, seeking to find out how the other half lived. And at once they shut up like clams. I was not of their kind; my speech had changed, the tones of my voice were different, in short, I was a superior, and they were superbly class conscious.

'What will you have?' I asked, as the waiter came for the order.

'Two slices an' a cup of tea,' meekly said the Carter.

'Two slices an' a cup of tea,' meekly said the Carpenter.

Stop a moment, and consider the situation. Here were two men, invited by me into the coffee-house. They had seen my gold piece, and they could understand that I was no pauper. One had eaten a ha'penny roll that day, the other had eaten nothing. And they called for 'two slices an' a cup of tea!' Each man had given a tu'penny order. 'Two slices', by the way, means two slices of bread and butter.

40

This was the same degraded humility that had characterized their attitude towards the poorhouse porter. But I wouldn't have it. Step by step I increased their orders – eggs, rashers of bacon, more eggs, more bacon, more tea, more slices and so forth – they denying wistfully all the while that they cared for anything more and devouring it ravenously as fast as it arrived.

'First cup o' tea I've 'ad in a fortnight,' said the Carter.

'Wonderful tea, that,' said the Carpenter.

They each drank two pints of it, and I assure you that it was slops. It resembled tea less than lager beer resembles champagne. Nay, it was 'water-bewitched', and did not resemble tea at all.

It was curious, after the first shock, to notice the effect the food had on them. At first they were melancholy, and talked of the divers times they had contemplated suicide. The Carter, not a week before, had stood on the bridge and looked at the water and pondered the question. Water, the Carter insisted, with heat, was a bad route. He, for one, he knew, would struggle. A bullet was ''andier', but how under the sun was he to get hold of a revolver? That was the rub.

They grew more cheerful as the hot 'tea' soaked in, and talked more about themselves. The Carter had buried his wife and children, with the exception of one son, who grew to manhood and helped him in his little business. Then the thing happened. The son, a man of thirty-one, died of the smallpox. No sooner was this over than the father came down with the fever and went to the hospital for three months. Then he was done for. He came out weak, debilitated, no strong young son to stand by him, his little business gone glimmering, and not a farthing. The thing had happened, and the game was up. No chance for an old man to start again. Friends all poor and unable to help. He had tried for work when they were putting up the stands for the first Coronation parade. 'An' I got fair sick of the answer: "No! no! no!" It rang in my ears at night when I tried to sleep, always the same, "No! no! no!"' Only the past week he had answered an advertisement in Hackney, and on giving his age was told, 'Oh, too old, too old by far.'

The Carpenter had been born in the army, where his father had served twenty-two years. Likewise, his two brothers had gone into the army; one, troop sergeant-major of the Seventh Hussars, dying in India after the Mutiny; the other, after nine years under Roberts in the East, had been lost in Egypt. The Carpenter had not gone into the army, so here he was, still on the planet.

'But 'ere, give me your 'and,' he said, ripping open his ragged shirt. 'I'm fit for the anatomist, that's all. I'm wastin' away sir, actually wastin' away for want of food. Feel my ribs an' you'll see.'

I put my hand under his shirt and felt. The skin was stretched like parchment over the bones, and the sensation produced was for all the world like running one's hand over a wash-board.

'Seven years o' bliss I 'ad,' he said. 'A good missus and three bonnie lassies. But they all died. Scarlet fever took the girls inside a fortnight.'

'After this, sir,' said the Carter, indicating the spread, and desiring to turn the conversation into more cheerful channels; 'after this, I wouldn't be able to eat a workhouse breakfast in the morning.'

'Nor I,' agreed the Carpenter, and they fell to discussing belly delights and the fine dishes their respective wives had cooked in the old days.

'I've gone three days and never broke my fast,' said the Carter.

'And I, five,' his companion added, turning gloomy with the memory of it. 'Five days once, with nothing on my stomach but a bit of orange peel, an' outraged nature wouldn't stand it, sir, an' I near died. Sometimes, walkin' the streets at night, I've ben that desperate I've made up my mind to win the horse or lose the saddle. You know what I mean, sir – to commit some big robbery. But when mornin' come, there was I, too weak from 'unger an' cold to 'arm a mouse.'

As their poor vitals warmed to the food, they began to expand and wax boastful, and to talk politics. I can only say that they talked politics as well as the average middle-class man, and a great deal better than some of the middle-class men I have heard. What surprised me was the hold they had on the world, its geography and peoples, and on recent and contemporaneous history. As I say, they were not fools, these two men. They were merely old, and their children had undutifully failed to grow up and give them a place by the fire.

One last incident, as I bade them good-bye on the corner, happy with a couple of shillings in their pockets and the certain prospect of a bed for the night. Lighting a cigarette, I was about to throw away the burning match when the Carter reached for it. I proffered him the box, but he said, 'Never mind, won't waste it, sir.' And while he lighted the cigarette I had given him, the Carpenter hurried with the filling of his pipe in order to have a go at the same match.

'It's wrong to waste,' said he.

'Yes,' I said, but I was thinking of the wash-board ribs over which I had run my hand.

CHAPTER NINE

THE SPIKE

FIRST of all, I must beg forgiveness of my body for the vileness through which I have dragged it, and forgiveness of my stomach for the vileness which I have thrust into it. I have been to the spike, and slept in the spike, and eaten in the spike; also, I have run away from the spike.

After my two unsuccessful attempts to penetrate the Whitechapel casual ward, I started early, and joined the desolate line before three o'clock in the afternoon. They did not 'Let in' till six, but at that early hour I was number twenty, while the news had gone forth that only twenty-two were to be admitted. By four o'clock there were thirty-four in line, the last ten hanging on in the slender hope of getting in by some kind of a miracle. Many more came, looked at the line, and went away, wise to the bitter fact that the spike would be 'full up'.

Conversation was slack at first, standing there, till the man on one side of me and the man on the other side of me discovered that they had been in the smallpox hospital at the same time, though a full house of sixteen hundred patients had prevented their becoming acquainted. But they made up for it, discussing and comparing the more loathsome features of their disease in the most cold-blooded, matter-of-fact way. I learned that the average mortality was one in six, that one of them had been in three months and the other three months and a half, and that they had been 'rotten wi' it'. Whereat my flesh began to creep and crawl, and I asked them how long they had been out. One had been out two weeks, and the other three weeks. Their faces were badly pitted (though each assured the other that this was not so), and further they showed me in their hands and under the nails the smallpox 'seeds' still working out. Nay, one of them worked a seed out for my edification, and pop it went, right out of his flesh into the air. I tried to shrink up smaller inside my clothes, and I registered a fervent though silent hope that it had not popped on me.

In both instances, I found that the smallpox was the cause of their being 'on the doss', which means on the tramp. Both had been working when smitten by the disease, and both had emerged from the hospital 'broke', with the gloomy task before them of hunting for work. So far, they had not found any, and they had come to the spike for a 'rest up' after three days and nights on the streets.

It seems that not only the man who becomes old is punished for his involuntary misfortune, but likewise the man who is struck by disease or accident. Later on, I talked with another man – 'Ginger' we called him – who stood at the head of the line – a sure indication that he had been waiting since one o'clock. A year before, one day, while in the employ of a fish dealer, he was carrying a heavy box of fish which was too much for him. Result: 'something broke', and there was the box on the ground, and he on the ground beside it.

At the first hospital, whither he was immediately carried, they said it was a rupture, reduced the swelling, gave him some vaseline to rub on it, kept him four hours, and told him to get along. But he was not on the streets more than two or three hours when he was down on his back again. This time he went to another hospital and was patched up. But the point is, the employer did nothing, positively nothing, for the man injured in his employment, and even refused him 'a light job now and again', when he came out. As far as Ginger is concerned, he is a broken man. His only chance to earn a living was by heavy work. He is now incapable of performing heavy work, and from now until he dies, the spike, the peg, and the streets are all he can look forward to in the way of food and shelter. The thing happened – that is all. He put his back under too great a load of fish, and his chance for happiness in life was crossed off the books.

Several men in the line had been to the United States, and they were wishing that they had remained there, and were cursing themselves for their folly in ever having left. England had become a prison to them, a prison from which there was no hope of escape. It was impossible for them to get away. They could neither scrape together the passage money, nor get a chance to work their passage. The country was too overrun by poor devils who built their 'lay'.

I was on the seafaring-man-who-had-lost-his-clothes-and-money tack, and they all condoled with me and gave me much sound advice. To sum it up, the advice was something like this: To keep out of all places like the spike. There was nothing good in it for me. To head for the coast and bend every effort to get away on a ship. To go to work, if possible, and scrape together a pound or so, with which I might bribe some steward or underling to give me chance to work my passage. They envied me my youth and strength, which would sooner or later get me out of the country. These they no longer possessed. Age and English hardship had broken them, and for them the game was played and up.

There was one, however, who was still young, and who, I am sure, will in the end make it out. He had gone to the United States as a young fellow, and in fourteen years' residence the longest period he had been out of work was twelve hours. He had saved his money, grown too prosperous, and returned to the mother-country. Now he was standing in line at the spike.

For the past two years, he told me, he had been working as a cook. His hours had been from 7 a.m. to 10.30 p.m., and on Saturday to 12.30 p.m. – ninety-five hours per week, for which he had received twenty shillings, or five dollars.

'But the work and the long hours was killing me,' he said, 'and I had to chuck the job. I had a little money saved, but I spent it living and looking for another place.'

This was his first night in the spike, and he had come in only to get rested. As soon as he emerged he intended to start for Bristol, a one-hundred-and-ten-mile walk, where he thought he would eventually get a ship for the States.

But the men in the line were not all of this calibre. Some were poor, wretched beasts, inarticulate and callous, but for all that, in many ways very human. I remember a carter, evidently returning home after the day's work, stopping his cart before us so that his young hopeful, who had run to meet him, could climb in. But the cart was big, the young hopeful little, and he failed in his several attempts to swarm up. Whereupon one of the most degraded-looking men stepped out of the line and hoisted him in. Now the virtue and the joy of this act lies in that it was service of love, not hire. The carter was poor, and the man knew it; and the man was standing in the spike line, and the carter knew it; and the man had done the little act, and the carter had thanked him, even as you and I would have done and thanked.

Another beautiful touch was that displayed by the 'Hopper' and his 'ole woman'. He had been in line about half an hour when the

44

THE "SPIKE"—WAITING OUTSIDE WHITECHAPEL WORKHOUSE

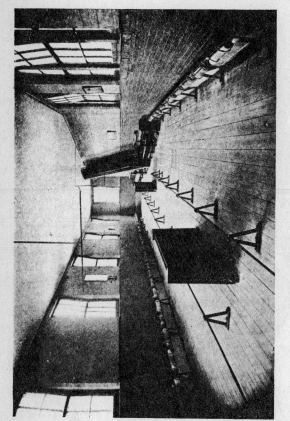

CASUAL WARD, WHITECHAPEL WORKHOUSE

the mistake of tardiness. Seven o'clock in the evening is too late in the day for a pauper to get a pauper's bed.

For the benefit of gently nurtured and innocent folk, let me explain what a casual ward is. It is a building where the homeless, bedless, penniless man, if he be lucky, may *casually* rest his weary bones, and then work like a navvy next day to pay for it.

My second attempt to break into the casual ward began more auspiciously. I started in the middle of the afternoon, accompanied by the burning young socialist and another friend, and all I had in my pocket was thru'pence. They piloted me to the Whitechapel Workhouse, at which I peered from around a friendly corner. It was a few minutes past five in the afternoon, but already a long and melancholy line was formed, which strung out around the corner of the building and out of sight.

It was a most woeful picture, men and women waiting in the cold grey end of the day for a pauper's shelter from the night, and I confess it almost unnerved me. Like the boy before the dentist's door, I suddenly discovered a multitude of reasons for being elsewhere. Some hints of the struggle going on within must have shown in my face, for one of my companions said, 'don't funk; you can do it.'

Of course I could do it, but I became aware that even thru'pence in my pocket was too lordly a treasure for such a throng; and, in order that all invidious distinctions might be removed, I emptied out the coppers. Then I bade good-bye to my friends, and with my heart going pit-a-pat, slouched down the street and took my place at the end of the line. Woeful it looked, this line of poor folk tottering on the steep pitch to death; how woeful it was I did not dream.

Next to me stood a short, stout man. Hale and hearty, though aged, strong-featured, with the tough and leathery skin produced by long years of sunbeat and weatherbeat, his was the unmistakable sea face and eyes; and at once there came to me a bit of Kipling's 'Galley Slave':

By the brand upon my shoulder, by the gall of clinging steel;
By the welt the whips have left me, by the scars that never heal;
By eyes grown old with staring through the sun-wash on the brine,
I am paid in full for service....

How correct I was in my surmise, and how peculiarly appropriate the verse was, you shall learn.

'I won't stand it much longer, I won't,' he was complaining to the man on the other side of him. 'I'll smash a windy, a big 'un, an' get run in for fourteen days. Then I'll have a good place to sleep, never fear, an' better grub than you get here. Though I'd miss my bit of baccy' – this as an after-thought, and said regretfully and resignedly.

'I've been out two nights now,' he went on; 'wet to the skin night before last, an' I can't stand it much longer. I'm gettin' old, an' some mornin' they'll pick me up dead.'

He whirled with fierce passion on me: 'Don't you ever let yourself grow old, lad. Die when you're young, or you'll come to this. I'm tellin' you sure. Seven an' eighty years am I, an' served my country like a man. Three good-conduct stripes and the Victoria Cross, an' this is what I get for it. I wish I was dead, I wish I was dead. Can't come any too quick for me, I tell you.'

The moisture rushed into his eyes, but, before the other man could comfort him, he began to hum a lilting sea song as though there was no such thing as heartbreak in the world.

Given encouragement, this is the story he told while waiting in line at the workhouse after two nights of exposure in the streets.

As a boy he had enlisted in the British navy, and for two score years and more served faithfully and well. Names, dates, commanders, ports, ships, engagements, and battles, rolled from his lips in a steady stream, but it is beyond me to remember them all, for it is not quite in keeping to take notes at the poorhouse door. He had been through the 'First War in China', as he termed it; had enlisted with the East India Company and served ten years in India; was back in India again, in the English navy at the time of the Mutiny; had served in the Burmese War and in the Crimea; and all this in addition to having fought and toiled for the English flag pretty well over the rest of the globe.

Then the thing happened. A little thing, if it could only be traced back to first causes: perhaps the lieutenant's breakfast had not agreed with him; or he had been up late the night before; or his debts were pressing; or the commander had spoken brusquely to him. The point is, that on this particular day the lieutenant was irritable. The sailor, with others, was 'setting up' the fore rigging.

Now, mark you, the sailor had been over forty years in the navy, had three good-conduct stripes, and possessed the Victoria Cross for distinguished service in battle; so he could not have been such an altogether bad sort of a sailorman. The lieutenant was irritable; the lieutenant called him a name – well, not a nice sort of name. It referred to his mother. When I was a boy it was our boys' code to fight like little demons should such an insult be given our mothers; and many men have died in my part of the world for calling other men this name.

However, the lieutenant called the sailor this name. At that moment it chanced the sailor had an iron lever or bar in his hands. He promptly struck the lieutenant over the head with it, knocking him out of the rigging and overboard.

And then, in the man's own words: 'I saw what I had done. I knew the Regulations, and I said to myself, "It's all up with you, Jack, my boy; so here goes." An' I jumped over after him, my mind made up to drown us both. An' I'd ha' done it, too, only the pinnace from the flag-ship was just comin' alongside. Up we came to the top, me a hold of him an' punchin' him. This was what settled for me. If I hadn't ben strikin' him, I could have claimed that, seein' what I had done, I jumped over to save him.'

Then came the court-martial, or whatever name a sea trial goes by. He recited his sentence, word for word, as though memorized and gone over in bitterness many times. And here it is, for the sake of discipline and respect to officers not always gentlemen, the

34

punishment of a man who was guilty of manhood. To be reduced to the rank of ordinary seaman; to be debarred all prize-money due him; to forfeit all rights to pension; to resign the Victoria Cross; to be discharged from the navy with a good character (this being his first offence); to receive fifty lashes; and to serve two years in prison.

'I wish I had drowned that day, I wish to God I had,' he concluded, as the line moved up and we passed around the corner.

At last the door came in sight, through which the paupers were being admitted in bunches. And here I learned a surprising thing: *this being Wednesday, none of us would be released till Friday morning.* Furthermore, and oh, you tobacco users, take heed: *we would not be permitted to take in any tobacco.* This we would have to surrender as we entered. Sometimes, I was told, it was returned on leaving and sometimes it was destroyed.

The old man-of-war's man gave me a lesson. Opening his pouch, he emptied the tobacco (a pitiful quantity) into a piece of paper. This, snugly and flatly wrapped, went down his sock inside his shoe. Down went my piece of tobacco inside my sock, for forty hours without tobacco is a hardship all tobacco users will understand.

Again and again the line moved up, and we were slowly but surely approaching the wicket. At the moment we happened to be standing on an iron grating, and a man appearing underneath, the old sailor called down to him,

'How many more do they want?'

'Twenty-four,' came the answer.

We looked ahead anxiously and counted. Thirty-four were ahead of us. Disappointment and consternation dawned upon the faces about me. It is not a nice thing, hungry and penniless, to face a sleepless night in the streets. But we hoped against hope, till, when ten stood outside the wicket, the porter turned us away.

'Full up,' was what he said, as he banged the door.

Like a flash, for all his eighty-seven years, the old sailor was speeding away on the desperate chance of finding shelter elsewhere. I stood and debated with two other men, wise in the knowledge of casual wards, as to where we should go. They decided on the Poplar Workhouse, three miles away, and we started off.

As we rounded the corner, one of them said, 'I could a' got in 'ere today. I come by at one o'clock, an' the line was beginnin' to form then – pets, that's what they are. They let 'm in, the same ones, night upon night.'

CHAPTER EIGHT

THE CARTER AND THE CARPENTER

THE Carter with his clean-cut face, chin beard, and shaved upper lip, I should have taken in the United States for anything from a master workman to a well-to-do farmer. The Carpenter – well, I should have taken him for a carpenter. He looked it, lean and wiry, with shrewd, observant eyes, and hands that had grown twisted to the handles of tools through forty-seven years' work at the trade. The chief difficulty with these men was that they were old, and that their children, instead of growing up to take care of them, had died. Their years had told on them, and they had been forced out of the whirl of industry by the younger and stronger competitors who had taken their places.

These two men, turned away from the casual ward of Whitechapel Workhouse, were bound with me for Poplar Workhouse. Not much of a show, they thought, but to chance. it was all that remained to us. It was Poplar, or the streets and night. Both men were anxious for a bed, for they were 'about gone', as they phrased it. The Carter, fifty-eight years of age, had spent the last three nights without shelter or sleep, while the Carpenter, sixty-five years of age, had been out five nights.

But, O dear, soft people, full of meat and blood, with white beds and airy rooms waiting you each night, how can I make you know what it is to suffer as you would suffer if you spent a weary night on London's streets? Believe me, you would think a thousand centuries had come and gone before the east paled into dawn; you would shiver till you were ready to cry aloud with the pain of each aching muscle; and you would marvel that you could endure so much and live. Should you rest upon a bench, and your tired eyes close, depend upon it the policeman would rouse you and gruffly order you to 'move on'. You may rest upon the bench, and benches are few and far between; but if rest means sleep, on you must go, dragging your tired body through the endless streets. Should you, in desperate slyness seek some forlorn alley or dark passageway and lie down, the omnipresent policeman will rout you out just the same. It is his business to rout you out. It is a law of the powers that be that you should be routed out.

But when the dawn came, the nightmare over, you would hale you home to refresh yourself, and until you died you would tell the story of your adventure to groups of admiring friends. It would grow into a mighty story. Your little eight-hour night would become an Odyssey and you a Homer.

Not so with these homeless ones who walked to Poplar Workhouse with me. And there are thirty-five thousand of them, men and women, in London Town this night. Please don't remember it as you go to bed; if you are as soft as you ought to be you may not rest so well as usual. But for old men of sixty, seventy, and eighty, ill-fed, with neither meat nor blood, to greet the dawn unrefreshed, and to stagger through the day in mad search for crusts, with relentless night rushing down upon them again, and to do this five nights and days – O dear, soft people, full of meat and blood, how can you ever understand?

I walked up Mile End Road between the Carter and the Carpenter. Mile End Road is a wide thoroughfare, cutting the heart of East London, and there were tens of thousands of people abroad on it. I tell you this so that you may fully appreciate what I shall describe 'ole woman' (his mate) came up to him. She was fairly clad, for her class, with a weather-worn bonnet on her grey head and a sacking-covered bundle in her arms. As she talked to him, he reached forward, caught the one stray wisp of the white hair that was flying wild, deftly twirled it between his fingers, and tucked it back properly behind her ear. From all of which one may conclude many things. He certainly liked her well enough to wish her to be neat and tidy. He was proud of her, standing there in the spike line, and it was his desire that she should look well in the eyes of the other unfortunates who stood in the spike line. But last and best, and underlying all these motives, it was a sturdy affection he bore her; for man is not prone to bother his head over neatness and tidiness in a woman for whom he does not care, nor is he likely to be proud of such a woman.

And I found myself questioning why this man and his mate, hard workers I knew from their talk, should have to seek a pauper lodging. He had pride, pride in his old woman and pride in himself. When I asked him what he thought I, a greenhorn, might expect to earn at 'hopping', he sized me up, and said that it all depended. Plenty of people were too slow to pick hops and made a failure of it. A man, to succeed, must use his head and be quick with his fingers, must be exceeding quick with his fingers. Now he and his old woman could do very well at it, working the one bin between them and not going to sleep over it; but then, they had been at it for years.

'I 'ad a mate as went down last year,' spoke up a man. 'It was 'is fust time, but 'e come back wi' two poun' ten in 'is pockit, an' 'e was only gone a month.'

'There you are,' said the Hopper, a wealth of admiration in his voice. ' 'E was quick. 'E was jest nat'rally born to it, 'e was.'

Two pound ten – twelve dollars and a half – for a month's work when one is 'jest nat'rally born to it!' And in addition, sleeping out without blankets and living the Lord knows how. There are moments when I am thankful that I was not 'jest nat'rally born' a genius for anything, not even hop-picking.

In the matter of getting an outfit for 'the hops', the Hopper gave me some sterling advice, to which same give heed, you soft and tender people, in case you should ever be stranded in London Town.

'If you ain't got tins an' cookin' things, all as you can get'll be bread and cheese. No bloomin' good that! You must 'ave 'ot tea, an' wegetables, an' a bit o' meat, now an' again, if you're goin' to do work as is work. Cawn't do it on cold wittles. Tell you wot you do, lad. Run around in the mornin' an' look in the dust pans. You'll find plenty o' tins to cook in. Fine tins, wonderful good some o' them. Me an' the ole woman got ours that way.' (He pointed at the bundle she held, while she nodded proudly, beaming on me with good-nature and consciousness of success and prosperity.) 'This overcoat is as good as a blanket,' he went on, advancing the skirt of it that I might feel its thickness 'An' 'oo knows, I may find a blanket before long.'

Again the old woman nodded and beamed, this time with the dead certainty that he *would* find a blanket before long.

'I call it a 'oliday, 'oppin',' he concluded rapturously. 'A tidy way o' gettin' two or three pounds together an' fixin' up for winter. The only thing I don't like' – and here was the rift within the lute – 'is paddin the 'oof down there.'

It was plain the years were telling on this energetic pair, and while they enjoyed the quick work with the fingers, 'paddin' the 'oof', which is walking, was beginning to bear heavily upon them. And I looked at their grey hairs, and ahead into the future ten years, and wondered how it would be with them.

I noticed another man and his old woman join the line, both of them past fifty. The woman, because she was a woman, was admitted into the spike; but he was too late, and, separated from his mate, was turned away to tramp the streets all night.

The street on which we stood, from wall to wall, was barely twenty feet wide. The sidewalks were three feet wide. It was a residence street. At least workmen and their families existed in some sort of fashion in the houses across from us. And each day and every day, from one in the afternoon till six, our ragged spike line is the principal feature of the view commanded by their front doors and windows. One workman sat in his door directly opposite us, taking his rest and a breath of air after the toil of the day. His wife came to chat with him. The doorway was too small for two, so she stood up. Their babes sprawled before them. And here was the spike line, less than a score of feet away – neither privacy for the workman, nor privacy for the pauper. About our feet played the children of the neighbourhood. To them our presence was nothing unusual. We were not an intrusion. We were as natural and ordinary as the brick walls and stone curbs of their environment. They had been born to the sight of the spike line, and all their brief days they had seen it.

At six o'clock the line moved up, and we were admitted in groups of three. Name, age, occupation, place of birth, condition of destitution, and the previous night's 'doss', were taken with lightning-like rapidity by the superintendent; and as I turned I was startled by a man's thrusting into my hand something that felt like a brick, and shouting into my ear, 'any knives, matches, or tobacco?' 'No, sir,' I lied, as lied every man who entered. As I passed downstairs to the cellar, I looked at the brick in my hand, and saw that by doing violence to the language, it might be called 'bread'. By its weight and hardness it certainly must have been unleavened.

The light was very dim down in the cellar, and before I knew it some other man had thrust a pannikin into my other hand. Then I stumbled on to a still darker room, where were benches and tables and men. The place smelled vilely, and the sombre gloom, and the mumble of voices from out of the obscurity, made it seem more like some anteroom to the infernal regions.

Most of the men were suffering from tired feet, and they prefaced the meal by removing their shoes and unbinding the filthy rags with

46

which their feet were wrapped. This added to the general noisomeness, while it took away from my appetite.

In fact, I found that I had made a mistake. I had eaten a hearty dinner five hours before, and to have done justice to the fare before me I should have fasted for a couple of days. The pannikin contained skilly, three-quarters of a pint, a mixture of Indian corn and hot water. The men were dipping their bread into heaps of salt scattered over the dirty tables. I attempted the same, but the bread seemed to stick in my mouth, and I remembered the words of the Carpenter, 'You need a pint of water to eat the bread nicely.'

I went over into a dark corner where I had observed other men going and found the water. Then I returned and attacked the skilly. It was coarse of texture, unseasoned, gross, and bitter. This bitterness which lingered persistently in the mouth after the skilly had passed on, I found especially repulsive. I struggled manfully, but was mastered by my qualms, and half-a-dozen mouthfuls of skilly and bread was the measure of my success. The man beside me ate his own share, and mine to boot, scraped the pannikins, and looked hungrily for more.

'I met a "towny", and he stood me too good a dinner,' I explained.

'An' I 'aven't 'ad a bite since yesterday mornin',' he replied.

'How about tobacco?' I asked. 'Will the bloke bother with a fellow now?'

'Oh no,' he answered me. 'No bloomin' fear. This is the easiest spike goin'. Y'oughto see some of them. Search you to the skin.'

The pannikins scraped clean, conversation began to spring up. 'This super'tendent 'ere is always writin' to the papers 'bout us mugs,' said the man on the other side of me.

'What does he say?' I asked.

'Oh, 'e sez we're no good, a lot o' blackguards an' scoundrels as won't work. Tells all the ole tricks I've been 'earin' for twenty years, an' w'ich I never seen a mug ever do. Las' thing of 'is I see, 'e was tellin' 'ow a mug gets out o' the spike, wi' a crust in 'is pockit. An' w'en 'e sees a nice ole gentleman comin' along the street 'e chucks the crust into the drain, an' borrows the old gent's stick to poke it out. An' then the ole gent gi'es 'im a tanner.'

A roar of applause greeted the time-honoured yarn, and from somewhere over in the deeper darkness came another voice, orating angrily:

'Talk o' the country bein' good for tommy [food]; I'd like to see it. I jest came up from Dover, an' blessed little tommy I got. They won't gi' ye a drink o' water, they won't, much less tommy.'

'There's mugs never go out of Kent,' spoke a second voice, 'an' they live bloomin' fat all along.'

'I come through Kent,' went on the first voice, still more angrily, 'an' Gawd blimey if I see any tommy. An' I always notices as the blokes as talks about 'ow much they can get, w'en they're in the spike can eat my share o' skilly as well as their bleedin' own.'

'There's chaps in London,' said a man across the table from me, 'that get all the tommy they want, an' they never think o' goin' to

47

the country. Stay in London the year 'round. Nor do they think of lookin' for a kip [place to sleep], till nine or ten o'clock at night.'

A general chorus verified this statement.

'But they're bloomin' clever, them chaps,' said an admiring voice. 'Course they are,' said another voice. 'But it's not the likes of me an' you can do it. You got to be born to it, I say. Them chaps 'ave ben openin' cabs an' sellin' papers since the day they was born, an' their fathers an' mothers before 'em. It's all in the trainin', I say, an' the likes of me an' you 'ud starve at it.'

This also was verified by the general chorus, and likewise the statement that there were 'mugs as lives the twelve-month 'round in the spike an' never get a blessed bit o' tommy other than spike skilly an' bread'.

'I once got arf a crown in the Stratford spike,' said a new voice. Silence fell on the instant, and all listened to the wonderful tale. 'There was three of us breakin' stones. Winter-time, an' the cold was cruel. T'other two said they'd be blessed if they do it, an' they didn't; but I kept wearin' into mine to warm up, you know. An' then the guardians come, an' t'other chaps got run in for fourteen days, an' the guardians, w'en they see wot I'd been doin', gives me a tanner each, five o' them, an' turns me up.'

The majority of these men, nay, all of them, I found, do not like the spike, and only come to it when driven in. After the 'rest up' they are good for two or three days and nights on the streets, when they are driven in again for another rest. Of course, this continuous hardship quickly breaks their constitutions, and they realize it, though only in a vague way; while it is so much the common run of things that they do not worry about it.

'On the doss', they call vagabondage here, which corresponds to 'on the road' in the United States. The agreement is that kipping, or dossing, or sleeping, is the hardest problem they have to face, harder even than that of food. The inclement weather and the harsh laws are mainly responsible for this, while the men themselves ascribe their homelessness to foreign immigration, especially of Polish and Russian Jews, who take their places at lower wages and establish the sweating system.

By seven o'clock we were called away to bathe and go to bed. We stripped our clothes, wrapping them up in our coats and buckling our belts about them, and deposited them in a heaped rack and on the floor – a beautiful scheme for the spread of vermin. Then, two by two, we entered the bathroom. There were two ordinary tubs, and this I know: the two men preceding had washed in that water, we washed in the same water, and it was not changed for the two men that followed us. This I know, but I am also certain that the twenty-two of us washed in the same water.

I did no more than make a show of splashing some of this dubious liquid at myself, while I hastily brushed it off with a towel wet from the bodies of other men. My equanimity was not restored by seeing the back of one poor wretch a mass of blood from attacks of vermin and retaliatory scratching.

48

A shirt was handed me – which I could not help but wonder how many other men had worn; and with a couple of blankets under my arm I trudged off to the sleeping apartment. This was a long, narrow room, traversed by two low iron rails. Between these rails were stretched, not hammocks, but pieces of canvas, six feet long and less then two feet wide. These were the beds, and they were six inches apart and about eight inches above the floor. The chief difficulty was that the head was somewhat higher than the feet, which caused the body constantly to slip down. Being slung to the same rails, when one man moved, no matter how slightly, the rest were set rocking; and whenever I dozed somebody was sure to struggle back to the position from which he had slipped, and arouse me again.

Many hours passed before I won to sleep. It was only seven in the evening, and the voices of children, in shrill outcry, playing in the street, continued till nearly midnight. The smell was frightful and sickening, while my imagination broke loose, and my skin crept and crawled till I was nearly frantic. Grunting, groaning, and snoring arose like the sounds emitted by some sea monster, and several times, afflicted by nightmare, one or another, by his shrieks and yells, aroused the lot of us. Towards morning I was awakened by a rat or some similar animal on my breast. In the quick transition from sleep to waking, before I was completely myself, I raised a shout to wake the dead. At any rate, I woke the living, and they cursed me roundly for my lack of manners.

But morning came, with a six o'clock breakfast of bread and skilly, which I gave away, and we were told off to our various tasks. Some were set to scrubbing and cleaning, others to picking oakum, and eight of us were convoyed across the street to the Whitechapel Infirmary, where we were set at scavenger work. This was the method by which we paid for our skilly and canvas, and I, for one, know that I paid in full many times over.

Though we had most revolting tasks to perform, our allotment was considered the best, and the other men deemed themselves lucky in being chosen to perform it.

'Don't touch it, mate, the nurse sez it's deadly,' warned my working partner, as I held open a sack into which he was emptying a garbage can.

It came from the sick wards, and I told him that I purposed neither to touch *it*, nor allow *it* to touch me. Nevertheless, I had to carry the sack, and other sacks, down five flights of stairs and empty them in a receptacle where the corruption was speedily sprinkled with strong disinfectant.

Perhaps there is a wise mercy in all this. These men of the spike, the peg, and the street, are encumbrances. They are of no good or use to any one, nor to themselves. They clutter the earth with their presence, and are better out of the way. Broken by hardship, ill fed, and worse nourished, they are always the first to be struck down by disease, as they are likewise the quickest to die.

They feel, themselves, that the forces of society tend to hurl them

49

out of existence. We were sprinkling disinfectant by the mortuary, when the dead waggon drove up and five bodies were packed into it. The conversation turned to the 'white potion' and 'black jack', and I found they were all agreed that the poor person, man or woman, who in the Infirmary gave too much trouble or was in a bad way, was 'polished off'. That is to say, the incurables and the obstreperous were given a dose of 'black jack' or the 'white potion', and sent over the divide. It does not matter in the least whether this be actually so or not. The point is, they have the feeling that it is so, and they have created the language with which to express that feeling – 'black jack', 'white potion', 'polishing off'.

At eight o'clock we went down into a cellar under the infirmary, where tea was brought to us, and the hospital scraps. These were heaped high on a huge platter in an indescribable mess – pieces of bread, chunks of grease and fat pork, the burnt skin from the outside of roasted joints, bones, in short, all the leavings from the fingers and mouths of the sick ones suffering from all manner of diseases. Into this mess the men plunged their hands, digging, pawing, turning over, examining, rejecting, and scrambling for. It wasn't pretty. Pigs couldn't have done worse. But the poor devils were hungry, and they ate ravenously of the swill, and when they could eat no more they bundled what was left into their handkerchiefs and thrust it inside their shirts.

'Once, w'en I was 'ere before, wot did I find out there but a 'ole lot of pork-ribs,' said Ginger to me. By 'out there' he meant the place where the corruption was dumped and sprinkled with strong disinfectant. 'They was a prime lot, no end o' meat on 'em, an' I 'ad 'em into my arms an' was out the gate an' down the street, a-lookin' for some 'un to gi' 'em to. Couldn't see a soul, an' I was runnin' round clean crazy, the bloke runnin' after me an' thinkin' I was "slingin' my 'ook" [running away]. But jest before 'e got me, I got a ole woman an' poked 'em into 'er apron.'

O Charity, O Philanthropy, descend to the spike and take a lesson from Ginger. At the bottom of the Abyss he performed as purely an altruistic act as was ever performed outside the Abyss. It was fine of Ginger, and if the old woman caught some contagion from the 'no end o' meat' on the pork-ribs, it was still fine, though not so fine. But the most salient thing in this incident, it seems to me, is poor Ginger, 'clean crazy' at sight of so much food going to waste.

It is the rule of the casual ward that a man who enters must stay two nights and a day; but I had seen sufficient for my purpose, had paid for my skilly and canvas, and was preparing to run for it.

'Come on, let's sling it,' I said to one of my mates, pointing towards the open gate through which the dead waggon had come.

'An' get fourteen days?'

'No; get away.'

'Aw, I come 'ere for a rest,' he said complacently. 'An' another night's kip won't 'urt me none.'

They were all of this opinion, so I was forced to 'sling it' alone.

'You cawn't ever come back 'ere again for a doss,' they warned me.

'No fear,' said I, with an enthusiasm they could not comprehend; and, dodging out the gate, I sped down the street.

Straight to my room I hurried, changed my clothes, and less than an hour from my escape, in a Turkish bath, I was sweating out whatever germs and other things had penetrated my epidermis, and wishing that I could stand a temperature of three hundred and twenty rather than two hundred and twenty.

CHAPTER TEN

CARRYING THE BANNER

'To carry the banner' means to walk the streets all night; and I, with the figurative emblem hoisted, went out to see what I could see. Men and women walk the streets at night all over this great city, but I selected the West End, making Leicester Square my base, and scouting about from the Thames Embankment to Hyde Park.

The rain was falling heavily when the theatres let out, and the brilliant throng which poured from the places of amusement was hard put to find cabs. The streets were so many wild rivers of cabs, most of which were engaged, however; and here I saw the desperate attempts of ragged men and boys to get a shelter from the night by procuring cabs for the cabless ladies and gentlemen. I used the word 'desperate' advisedly, for these wretched, homeless ones were gambling a soaking against a bed; and most of them, I took notice, got the soaking and missed the bed. Now, to go through a stormy night with wet clothes, and, in addition, to be ill nourished and not to have tasted meat for a week or a month, is about as severe a hardship as a man can undergo. Well fed and well clad, I have travelled all day with the spirit thermometer down to seventy-four degrees below zero – one hundred and six degrees of frost;* and though I suffered, it was a mere nothing compared with carrying the banner for a night, ill fed, ill clad, and soaking wet.

The streets grew very quiet and lonely after the theatre crowd had gone home. Only were to be seen the ubiquitous policemen, flashing their dark lanterns into doorways and alleys, and men and women and boys taking shelter in the lee of buildings from the wind and rain. Piccadilly, however, was not quite so deserted. Its pavements were brightened by well-dressed women without escort, and there was more life and action than elsewhere, due to the process of finding escort. But by three o'clock the last of them had vanished, and it was then indeed lonely.

At half past one the steady downpour ceased, and only showers fell thereafter. The homeless folk came away from the protection of the buildings, and slouched up and down and everywhere in order to rush up the circulation and keep warm.

One old woman, between fifty and sixty, a sheer wreck, I had noticed earlier in the night standing in Piccadilly, not far from

* This in the Klondike.—J.L.

Leicester Square. She seemed to have neither the sense nor the strength to get out of the rain or keep walking but stood stupidly, whenever she got the chance, meditating on past days, I imagine, when life was young and blood was warm. But she did not get the chance often. She was moved on by every policeman, and it required an average of six moves to send her doddering off one man's beat and on to another's. By three o'clock she had progressed as far as St. James's Street, and as the clocks were striking four I saw her sleeping soundly against the iron railings of Green Park. A brisk shower was falling at the time, and she must have been drenched to the skin.

Now, said I, at one o'clock, to myself; consider that you are a poor young man, penniless, in London Town, and that tomorrow you must look for work. It is necessary, therefore, that you get some sleep in order that you may have strength to look for work and to do work in case you find it.

So I sat down on the stone steps of a building. Five minutes later a policeman was looking at me. My eyes were wide open, so he only grunted and passed on. Ten minutes later my head was on my knees, I was dozing, and the same policeman was saying gruffly, ''Ere, you, get outa that!'

I got. And, like the old woman, I continued to get; for every time I dozed, a policeman was there to rout me along again. Not long after, when I had given this up, I was walking with a young Londoner (who had been out to the colonies and wished he were out to them again), when I noticed an open passage leading under a building and disappearing in darkness. A low iron gate barred the entrance. 'Come on,' I said. 'Let's climb over and get a good sleep.'

'Wot?' he answered, recoiling from me. 'An' get run in fer three months! Blimey if I do!'

Later on I was passing Hyde Park with a young boy of fourteen or fifteen, a most wretched-looking youth, gaunt and hollowed-eyed and sick.

'Let's go over the fence,' I proposed, 'and crawl into the shrubbery for a sleep. The bobbies couldn't find us there.'

'No fear,' he answered. 'There's the park guardians, and they'd run you in for six months.'

Times have changed, alas! When I was a youngster I used to read of homeless boys sleeping in doorways. Already the thing has become a tradition. As a stock situation it will doubtless linger in literature for a century to come, but as a cold fact it has ceased to be. Here are the doorways, and here are the boys, but happy conjunctions are no longer effected. The doorways remain empty, and the boys keep awake and carry the banner.

'I was down under the arches,' grumbled another young fellow. By 'arches' he meant the shore arches where begin the bridges that span the Thames. 'I was down under the arches w'en it was ryning its 'ardest, an' a bobby comes in an' chyses me out. But I come back, an' 'e come too. "'ere," sez 'e, "wot you doin' 'ere?" An' out I goes, but I sez, "Think I want ter pinch [steal] the bleedin' bridge?"'

52

Among those who carry the banner, Green Park has the reputation of opening its gates earlier than the other parks, and at quarter-past four in the morning, I, and many more, entered Green Park. It was raining again, but they were worn out with the night's walking, and they were down on the benches and asleep at once. Many of the men stretched out full length on the dripping wet grass, and, with the rain falling steadily upon them, were sleeping the sleep of exhaustion.

And now I wish to criticize the powers that be. They *are* the powers, therefore they may decree whatever they please; so I make bold only to criticize the ridiculousness of their decrees. All night long they make the homeless ones walk up and down. They drive them out of doors and passages, and lock them out of the parks. The evident intention of all this is to deprive them of sleep. Well and good, the powers have the power to deprive them of sleep, or of anything else for that matter; but why under the sun do they open the gates of the parks at five o'clock in the morning and let the homeless ones go inside and sleep? If it is their intention to deprive them of sleep, why do they let them sleep after five in the morning? And if it is not their intention to deprive them of sleep, why don't they let them sleep earlier in the night?

In this connection, I will say that I came by Green Park that same day, at one in the afternoon, and that I counted scores of the ragged wretches asleep in the grass. It was Sunday afternoon, the sun was fitfully appearing, and the well-dressed West Enders, with their wives and progeny, were out by thousands, taking the air. It was not a pleasant sight for them, those horrible, unkempt, sleeping vagabonds; while the vagabonds themselves, I know, would rather have done their sleeping the night before.

And so, dear soft people, should you ever visit London Town, and see these men asleep on the benches and in the grass, please do not think they are lazy creatures, preferring sleep to work. Know that the powers that be have kept them walking all the night long, and that in the day they have nowhere else to sleep.

CHAPTER ELEVEN

THE PEG

BUT, after carrying the banner all night, I did not sleep in Green Park when morning dawned. I was wet to the skin, it is true, and I had had no sleep for twenty-four hours; but, still adventuring as a penniless man looking for work, I had to look about me, first for a breakfast, and next for the work.

During the night I had heard of a place over on the Surrey side of the Thames, where the Salvation Army every Sunday morning gave away a breakfast to the unwashed. (And, by the way, the men who carry the banner *are* unwashed in the morning, and unless it is raining they do not have much show for a wash, either.) This, thought I, is the very thing – breakfast in the morning, and then the whole day in which to look for work.

It was a weary walk. Down St. James's Street I dragged my tired legs, along Pall Mall, past Trafalgar Square, to the Strand. I crossed the Waterloo Bridge to the Surrey side, cut across to Blackfriars Road, coming out near the Surrey Theatre, and arrived at the Salvation Army barracks before seven o'clock. This was 'the peg'. And by 'the peg', in the argot, is meant the place where a free meal may be obtained.

Here was a motley crowd of woebegone wretches who had spent the night in the rain. Such prodigious misery! and so much of it! Old men, young men, all manner of men, and boys to boot, and all manner of boys. Some were drowsing standing up; half a score of them were stretched out on the stone steps in most painful postures, all of them sound asleep, the skin of their bodies showing red through the holes and rents in their rags. And up and down the street and across the street for a block either way, each doorstep had from two to three occupants, all asleep, their heads bent forward on their knees. And, it must be remembered, these are not hard times in England. Things are going on very much as they ordinarily do, and times are neither hard nor easy.

And then came the policeman. 'Get outa that, you bloomin' swine! Eigh! eigh! Get out now!' And like swine he drove them from the doorways and scattered them to the four winds of Surrey. But when he encountered the crowd asleep on the steps he was astounded. 'Shocking!' he exclaimed. 'Shocking! And of a Sunday morning! A pretty sight! Eigh! eigh! Get outa that, you bleeding nuisances!'

Of course it was a shocking sight. I was shocked myself. And I should not care to have my own daughter pollute her eyes with such a sight, or come within half a mile of it; but – and there we were, and there you are, and 'but' is all that can be said.

The policeman passed on, and back we clustered, like flies around a honey jar. For was there not that wonderful thing, a breakfast awaiting us? We could not have clustered more persistently and desperately had they been giving away million-dollar bank-notes. Some were already off to sleep, when back came the policeman and away we scattered, only to return again as soon as the coast was clear.

At half past seven a little door opened, and a Salvation Army soldier stuck out his head. 'Ayn't no sense blockin' the wy up that wy,' he said. 'Those as 'as tickets cawn come hin now, an' those as 'asn't cawn't come hin till nine.'

Oh, that breakfast! Nine o'clock! An hour and a half longer! The men who held tickets were greatly envied. They were permitted to go inside, have a wash, and sit down and rest until breakfast, while we waited for the same breakfast on the street. The tickets had been distributed the previous night on the streets and along the Embankment, and the possession of them was not a matter of merit, but of chance.

At eight-thirty, more men with tickets were admitted, and by nine the little gate was opened to us. We crushed through somehow, and found ourselves packed in a courtyard like sardines. On more occasions than one, as a Yankee tramp in Yankeeland, I have had to work for my breakfast; but for no breakfast did I ever work so hard as for this one. For over two hours I had waited outside, and for over another hour I waited in this packed courtyard. I had had nothing to eat all night, and I was weak and faint, while the smell of the soiled clothes and unwashed bodies steaming from pent animal heat, and blocked solidly about me, nearly turned my stomach. So tightly were we packed, that a number of the men took advantage of the opportunity and went soundly asleep standing up.

Now, about the Salvation Army in general I know nothing, and whatever criticism I shall make here is of that particular portion of the Salvation Army which does business on Blackfriars Road near the Surrey Theatre. In the first place, this forcing of men who have been up all night to stand on their feet for hours longer, is as cruel as it is needless. We were weak, famished, and exhausted from our night's hardship and lack of sleep, and yet there we stood, and stood, and stood, without rhyme or reason.

Sailors were very plentiful in this crowd. It seemed to me that one man in four was looking for a ship, and I found at least a dozen of them to be American sailors. In accounting for their being 'on the beach', I received the same story from each and all, and from my knowledge of sea affairs this story rang true. English ships sign their sailors for the voyage, which means the round trip, sometimes lasting as long as three years; and they cannot sign off and receive their discharges until they reach the home port, which is England. Their wages are low, their food is bad, and their treatment worse. Very often they are really forced by their captains to desert in the New World or the colonies, leaving a handsome sum of wages behind them – a distinct gain, either to the captain or the owners, or to both. But whether for this reason alone or not, it is a fact that large numbers of them desert. Then, for the home voyage, the ship engages whatever sailors it can find on the beach. These men are engaged at the somewhat higher wages that obtain in other portions of the world, under the agreement that they shall sign off on reaching England. The reason for this is obvious; for it would be poor business policy to sign them for any longer time, since seamen's wages are low in England, and England is always crowded with sailormen on the beach. So this fully accounted for the American seamen at the Salvation Army barracks. To get off the beach in other outlandish places they had come to England, and gone on the beach in the most outlandish place of all.

There were fully a score of Americans in the crowd, the non-sailors being 'tramps royal', the men whose 'mate is the wind that tramps the world'. They were all cheerful, facing things with the pluck which is their chief characteristic and which seems never to desert them, withal they were cursing the country with lurid metaphors quite refreshing after a month of unimaginative monotonous Cockney swearing. The Cockney has one oath, and one

55

oath only, the most indecent in the language, which he uses on any and every occasion. Far different is the luminous and varied Western swearing, which runs to blasphemy rather than indecency. And after all, since men will swear, I think I prefer blasphemy to indecency; there is an audacity about it, an adventuresomeness and defiance that is better than sheer filthiness.

There was one American tramp royal whom I found particularly enjoyable. I first noticed him on the street, asleep in a doorway, his head on his knees, but a hat on his head that one does not meet this side of the Western Ocean. When the policeman routed him out, he got up slowly and deliberately, looked at the policeman, yawned and stretched himself, looked at the policeman again as much as to say he didn't know whether he would or wouldn't, and then sauntered leisurely down the sidewalk. At the outset I was sure of the hat, but this made me sure of the wearer of the hat.

In the jam inside I found myself alongside of him, and we had quite a chat. He had been through Spain, Italy, Switzerland, and France, and had accomplished the practically impossible feat of beating his way three hundred miles on a French railway without being caught at the finish. Where was I hanging out? he asked. And how did I manage for 'kipping'? – which means sleeping. Did I know the rounds yet? He was getting on, though the country was 'horstyl' and the cities were 'bum'. Fierce, wasn't it? Couldn't 'Batter' (beg) anywhere without being 'pinched'. But he wasn't going to quit it. Buffalo Bill's Show was coming over soon, and a man who could drive eight horses was sure of a job any time. These mugs over here didn't know beans about driving anything more than a span. What was the matter with me hanging on and waiting for Buffalo Bill? He was sure I could ring in somehow.

And so, after all, blood is thicker than water. We were fellow-countrymen and strangers in a strange land. I had warmed to his battered old hat at sight of it, and he was as solicitous for my welfare as if we were blood brothers. We swapped all manner of useful information concerning the country and the ways of its people, methods by which to obtain food and shelter and what not, and we parted genuinely sorry at having to say good-bye.

One thing particularly conspicuous in this crowd was the shortness of stature. I, who am but of medium height, looked over the heads of nine out of ten. The natives were all short, as were the foreign sailors. There were only five or six in the crowd who could be called fairly tall, and they were Scandinavians and Americans. The tallest man there, however, was an exception. He was an Englishman, though not a Londoner. 'Candidate for the Life Guards,' I remarked to him. 'You've hit it, mate,' was his reply; 'I've served my bit in that same, and the way things are I'll be back at it before long.'

For an hour we stood quietly in this packed courtyard. Then the men began to grow restless. There was pushing and shoving forward, and a mild hubbub of voices. Nothing rough, however, nor violent; merely the restlessness of weary and hungry men. At this juncture

THE SALVATION ARMY BARRACKS—WAITING

SALVATION ARMY BARRACKS—IN THE COURTYARD

forth came the adjutant. I did not like him. His eyes were not good.
There was nothing of the lowly Galilean about him, but a great deal
of the centurion who said: 'For I am a man in authority, having
soldiers under me; and I say to this man, Go, and he goeth; and
to another, Come, and he cometh; and to my servant, Do this, and
he doeth it.'

Well, he looked at us in just that way, and those nearest to him
quailed. Then he lifted his voice.

'Stop this 'ere, or I'll turn you the other wy an' march you out,
an' you'll get no breakfast.'

I cannot convey by printed speech the insufferable way in which
he said this. He seemed to me to revel in that he was a man
in authority, able to say to half a thousand ragged wretches, 'you
may eat or go hungry, as I elect'.

To deny us our breakfast after standing for hours! It was an
awful threat, and the pitiful abject silence which instantly fell
attested its awfulness. And it was a cowardly threat. We could not
strike back, for we were starving; and it is the way of the world that
when one man feeds another he is that man's master. But the
centurion – I mean the adjutant – was not satisfied. In the dead
silence he raised his voice again, and repeated the threat, and
amplified it.

At last we were permitted to enter the feasting hall, where we
found the 'ticket men' washed but unfed. All told, there must have
been nearly seven hundred of us who sat down – not to meat or
bread, but to speech, song, and prayer. From all of which I am
convinced that Tantalus suffers in many guises this side of the
infernal regions. The adjutant made the prayer, but I did not take
note of it, being too engrossed with the massed picture of misery
before me. But the speech ran something like this: 'You will feast
in Paradise. No matter how you starve and suffer here, you will
feast in Paradise, that is, if you will follow the directions.' And so
forth and so forth. A clever bit of propaganda, I took it, but rendered
of no avail for two reasons. First, the men who received it were
unimaginative and materialistic, unaware of the existence of any
Unseen, and too inured to hell on earth to be frightened by hell to
come. And second, weary and exhausted from the night's sleepless-
ness and hardship, suffering from the long wait upon their feet, and
faint from hunger, they were yearning, not for salvation, but for
grub. The 'soul-snatchers' (as these men call all religious propa-
gandists) should study the physiological basis of psychology a
little, if they wish to make their efforts more effective.

All in good time, about eleven o'clock, breakfast arrived. It arrived,
not on plates, but in paper parcels. I did not have all I wanted, and
I am sure that no man there had all he wanted, or half of what he
wanted or needed. I gave part of my bread to the tramp royal who
was waiting for Buffalo Bill, and he was as ravenous at the end as
he was in the beginning. This is the breakfast: two slices of bread,
one small piece of bread with raisins in it and called 'cake', a wafer
of cheese, and a mug of 'water bewitched'. Numbers of the men

had been waiting since five o'clock for it, while all of us had waited at least four hours; and in addition, we had been herded like swine, packed like sardines, and treated like curs, and been preached at, and sung to, and prayed for. Nor was that all.

No sooner was breakfast over (and it was over almost as quickly as it takes to tell), than the tired heads began to nod and droop, and in five minutes half of us were sound asleep. There were no signs of our being dismissed, while there were unmistakable signs of preparation for a meeting. I looked at a small clock hanging on the wall. It indicated twenty-five minutes to twelve. Heigh-ho, thought I, time is flying, and I have yet to look for work.

'I want to go,' I said to a couple of waking men near me.

'Got ter sty fer the service,' was the answer.

'Do you want to stay?' I asked.

They shook their heads.

'Then let us go and tell them we want to get out,' I continued. 'Come on.'

But the poor creatures were aghast. So I left them to their fate, and went up to the nearest Salvation Army man.

'I want to go,' I said. 'I came here for breakfast in order that I might be in shape to look for work. I didn't think it would take so long to get breakfast. I think I have a chance for work in Stepney, and the sooner I start, the better chance I'll have of getting it.'

He was really a good fellow, though he was startled by my request. 'Wy,' he said, 'we're goin' to 'old services, and you'd better sty.'

'But that will spoil my chances for work,' I urged. 'And work is the most important thing for me just now.'

As he was only a private, he referred me to the adjutant, and to the adjutant I repeated my reasons for wishing to go, and politely requested that he let me go.

'But it cawn't be done,' he said, waxing virtuously indignant at such ingratitude. 'The idea!' he snorted. 'The idea!'

'Do you mean to say that I can't get out of here?' I demanded. 'That you will keep me here against my will?'

'Yes,' he snorted.

I do not know what might have happened, for I was waxing indignant myself; but the 'congregation' had 'piped' the situation, and he drew me over to a corner of the room, and then into another room. Here he again demanded my reasons for wishing to go.

'I want to go,' I said, 'because I wish to look for work over in Stepney, and every hour lessens my chance of finding work. It is now twenty-five minutes to twelve. I did not think when I came in that it would take so long to get a breakfast.'

'You 'ave business, eh?' he sneered. 'A man of business you are, eh? Then wot did you come 'ere for?'

'I was out all night, and I needed a breakfast in order to strengthen me to find work. That is why I came here.'

'A nice thing to do,' he went on in the same sneering manner. 'A man with business shouldn't come 'ere. You've tyken some poor man's breakfast 'ere this morning, that's wot you've done.'

Which was a lie, for every mother's son of us had come in.

Now I submit, was this Christian-like, or even honest? – after I had plainly stated that I was homeless and hungry, and that I wished to look for work, for him to call my looking for work 'business', to call me therefore a business man, and to draw the corollary that a man of business, and well off, did not require a charity breakfast, and that by taking a charity breakfast I had robbed some hungry waif who was not a man of business.

I kept my temper, but I went over the facts again, and clearly and concisely demonstrated to him how unjust he was and how he had perverted the facts. As I manifested no signs of backing down (and I am sure my eyes were beginning to snap), he led me to the rear of the building, where, in an open court, stood a tent. In the same sneering tone he informed a couple of privates standing there that ' 'ere is a fellow that 'as business an' 'e wants to go before services.'

They were duly shocked, of course, and they looked unutterable horror while he went into the tent and brought out the major. Still in the same sneering manner, laying particular stress on the 'business', he brought my case before the commanding officer. The major was of a different stamp of man. I liked him as soon as I saw him, and to him I stated my case in the same fashion as before.

'Didn't you know you had to stay for services?' he asked.

'Certainly not,' I answered, 'or I should have gone without my breakfast. You have no placards posted to that effect, nor was I so informed when I entered the place.'

He meditated for a moment. 'You can go,' he said.

It was twelve o'clock when I gained the street, and I couldn't quite make up my mind whether I had been in the army or in prison. The day was half gone, and it was a far fetch to Stepney. And besides, it was Sunday, and why should even a starving man look for work on Sunday? Furthermore, it was my judgment that I had done a hard night's work walking the streets, and a hard day's work getting my breakfast; so I disconnected myself from my working hypothesis of a starving young man in search of employment, hailed a bus, and climbed aboard.

After a shave and a bath, with my clothes all off, I got in between clean white sheets and went to sleep. It was six in the evening when I closed my eyes. When they opened again, the clocks were striking nine next morning. I had slept fifteen straight hours. And as I lay there drowsily, my mind went back to the seven hundred unfortunates I had left waiting for services. No bath, no shave for them, no clean white sheets and all clothes off, and fifteen hours' straight sleep. Services over, it was the weary streets again, the problem of a crust of bread ere night, and the long sleepless night in the streets, and the pondering of the problem of how to obtain a crust at dawn.

CHAPTER TWELVE

CORONATION DAY

O thou that sea-walls sever
From lands unwalled by seas!
Wilt thou endure forever,
O Milton's England, these?
Thou that wast his Republic,
Wilt thou clasp their knees?
These royalties rust-eaten,
These worm-corroded lies
That keep thy head storm-beaten,
And sun-like strength of eyes
From the open air and heaven
Of intercepted skies!

SWINBURNE

VIVAT REX EDUARDUS! They crowned a king this day, and there has been great rejoicing and elaborate tomfoolery, and I am perplexed and saddened. I never saw anything to compare with the pageant, except Yankee circuses and Alhambra ballets; nor did I ever see anything so hopeless and so tragic.

To have enjoyed the Coronation procession, I should have come straight from America to the Hotel Cecil, and straight from the Hotel Cecil to a five-guinea seat among the washed. My mistake was in coming from the unwashed of the East End. There were not many who came from that quarter. The East End, as a whole, remained in the East End and got drunk. The Socialists, Democrats, and Republicans went off to the country for a breath of fresh air, quite unaffected by the fact that four hundred millions of people were taking to themselves a crowned and anointed ruler. Six thousand five hundred prelates, priests, statesmen, princes, and warriors beheld the crowning and anointing, and the rest of us the pageant as it passed.

I saw it at Trafalgar Square, 'the most splendid site in Europe', and the very innermost heart of the empire. There were many thousands of us, all checked and held in order by a superb display of armed power. The line of march was double-walled with soldiers. The base of the Nelson Column was triple-fringed with bluejackets. Eastward, at the entrance to the square, stood the Royal Marine Artillery. In the triangle of Pall Mall and Cockspur Street, the statue of George III was buttressed on either side by the Lancers and Hussars. To the west were the red-coats of the Royal Marines, and from the Union Club to the embouchure of Whitehall swept the glittering, massive curve of the 1st Life Guards – gigantic men mounted on gigantic chargers, steel-breastplated, steel-helmeted, steel-caparisoned, a great war-sword of steel ready to the hand of the powers that be. And further, throughout the crowd, were flung

60

long lines of the Metropolitan Constabulary, while in the rear were the reserves – tall, well-fed men, with weapons to wield and muscles to wield them in case of need.

And as it was thus at Trafalgar Square, so was it along the whole line of march – force, overpowering force; myriads of men, splendid men, the pick of the people, whose sole function in life is blindly to obey, and blindly to kill and destroy and stamp out life. And that they should be well fed, well clothed, and well armed, and have ships to hurl them to the ends of the earth, the East End of London, and the 'East End' of all England, toils and rots and dies.

There is a Chinese proverb that if one man lives in laziness another will die of hunger; and Montesquieu has said, 'The fact that many men are occupied in making clothes for one individual is the cause of there being many people without clothes.' So one explains the other. We cannot understand the starved and runty* toiler of the East End (living with his family in a one-room den, and letting out the floor space for lodgings to other starved and runty toilers) till we look at the strapping Life Guardsmen of the West End, and come to know that the one must feed and clothe and groom the other.

And while in Westminster Abbey the people were taking unto themselves a king, I, jammed between the Life Guards and Constabulary of Trafalgar Square, was dwelling upon the time when the people of Israel first took unto themselves a king. You all know how it runs. The elders came to the prophet Samuel, and said: 'Make us a king to judge us like all the nations.'

And the Lord said unto Samuel: Now therefore hearken unto their voice; howbeit thou shalt show them the manner of the king that shall reign over them.

And Samuel told all the words of the Lord unto the people that asked of him a king, and he said:

This will be the manner of the king that shall reign over you; he will take your sons, and appoint them unto him, for his chariots, and to be his horsemen, and they shall run before his chariots.

And he will appoint them unto him for captains of thousands, and captains of fifties; and he will set some to plough his ground, and to reap his harvest, and to make his instruments of war, and the instruments of his chariots.

And he will take your daughters to be confectionaries, and to be cooks, and to be bakers.

And he will take your fields, and your vineyards, and your oliveyards, even the best of them, and give them to his servants.

And he will take a tenth of your seed, and of your vineyards, and give to his officers, and to his servants.

And he will take your menservants, and your maidservants, and your goodliest young men, and your asses, and put them to his work.

* 'Runt' in America is the equivalent of the English 'crowl' the dwarf of a litter.

He will take a tenth of your flocks; and ye shall be his servants.

And ye shall call out in that day because of your king which ye shall have chosen you; and the Lord will not answer you in that day.

All of which came to pass in that ancient day, and they did cry out to Samuel, saying: 'Pray for thy servants unto the Lord thy God, that we die not; for we have added unto all our sins this evil, to ask us a king.' And after Saul, David, and Solomon, came Rehoboam, who answered the people roughly, saying: 'My father made your yoke heavy, but I will add to your yoke; my father chastised you with whips, but I will chastise you with scorpions.'

And in these latter days, five hundred hereditary peers own one-fifth of England; and they, and the officers and servants under the King, and those who go to compose the powers that be, yearly spend in wasteful luxury $1,850,000,000 or £370,000,000, which is thirty-two per cent of the total wealth produced by all the toilers of the country.

At the Abbey, clad in wonderful golden raiment, amid fanfare of trumpets and throbbing of music, surrounded by a brilliant throng of masters, lords, and rulers, the King was being invested with the insignia of his sovereignty. The spurs were placed to his heels by the Lord Great Chamberlain, and a sword of state, in purple scabbard, was presented him by the Archbishop of Canterbury, with these words:

Receive this kingly sword brought now from the altar of God, and delivered to you by the hands of the bishops and servants of God, though unworthy.

Whereupon, being girded, he gave heed to the Archbishop's exhortation:

With this sword do justice, stop the growth of iniquity, protect the Holy Church of God, help and defend widows and orphans, restore the things that are gone to decay, maintain the things that are restored, punish and reform what is amiss, and confirm what is in good order.

But hark! There is cheering down Whitehall; the crowd sways, the double walls of soldiers come to attention, and into view swing the King's watermen, in fantastic medieval garbs of red, for all the world like the van of a circus parade. Then a royal carriage, filled with ladies and gentlemen of the household with powdered footmen and coachmen most gorgeously arrayed. More carriages, lords and chamberlains, viscounts, mistresses of the robes – lackeys all. Then the warriors, a kingly escort, generals, bronzed and worn, from the ends of the earth come up to London Town, volunteer officers, officers of the militia and regular forces; Spens and Plumer, Broadwood and Cooper who relieved Ookiep, Mathias of Dargai, Dixon of Vlakfontein; General Gaselee and Admiral Seymour of China; Kitchener of Khartoum; Lord Roberts of India and all the world – the fighting men of England, masters of destruction, engineers of death! Another race of men from those of the shops and slums, a totally different race of men.

But here they come, in all the pomp and certitude of power, and still they come, these men of steel, these war lords and world harnessers. Pell-mell, peers and commoners, princes and maharajahs, Equerries to the King and Yeomen of the Guard. And here the colonials, lithe and hardy men; and here all the breeds of all the world – soldiers from Canada, Australia, New Zealand; from Bermuda, Borneo, Fiji, and the Gold Coast; from Rhodesia, Cape Colony, Natal, Sierra Leone and Gambia, Nigeria, and Uganda; from Ceylon, Cyprus, Hong Kong, Jamaica, and Wei-Hai-Wei; from Lagos, Malta, St. Lucia, Singapore, Trinidad. And here the conquered men of Ind, swarthy horsemen and sword wielders, fiercely barbaric, blazing in crimson and scarlet, Sikhs, Rajputs, Burmese, province by province, and caste by caste.

And now the Horse Guards, a glimpse of beautiful cream ponies, and a golden panoply, a hurricane of cheers, the crashing of bands – 'The King! the King! God save the King!' Everybody has gone mad. The contagion is sweeping me off my feet – I, too, want to shout, 'The King! God save the King!' Ragged men about me, tears in their eyes, are tossing up their hats and crying ecstatically, 'Bless 'em! Bless 'em! Bless 'em!' See, there he is, in that wondrous golden coach, the great crown flashing on his head, the woman in white beside him likewise crowned.

And I check myself with a rush, striving to convince myself that it is all real and rational, and not some glimpse of fairyland. This I cannot succeed in doing, and it is better so. I much prefer to believe that all this pomp, and vanity, and show, and mumbo-jumbo foolery has come from fairyland, than to believe it the performance of sane and sensible people who have mastered matter and solved the secrets of the stars.

Princes and princelings, dukes, duchesses, and all manner of coroneted folk of the royal train are flashing past; more warriors and lackeys, and conquered peoples, and the pageant is over. I drift with the crowd out of the square into a tangle of narrow streets, where the public-houses are a-roar with drunkenness, men, women, and children mixed together in colossal debauch. And on every side is rising the favourite song of the Coronation:

'Oh! on Coronation Day, on Coronation Day,
We'll have a spree, a jubilee, and shout, Hip, hip, hooray,
For we'll all be merry, drinking whisky, wine, and sherry,
We'll all be merry on Coronation Day.'

The rain is pouring down. Up the street come troops of the auxiliaries, black Africans and yellow Asiatics, beturbaned and befezed, and coolies swinging along with machine guns and mountain batteries on their heads, and the bare feet of all, in quick rhythm, going slish, slish, slish through the pavement mud. The public-houses empty by magic, and the swarthy allegiants are cheered by their British brothers, who return at once to the carouse.

'And how did you like the procession, mate?' I asked an old man on a bench in Green Park.

' 'Ow did I like it? A bloomin, good chawnce, sez I to myself, for a sleep, wi' all the coppers aw'y, so I turned into the corner there, along wi' fifty others. But I couldn't sleep, a'lyin' there 'ungry an' thinkin' 'ow I'd worked all the years o' my life an' now 'ad no plyce to rest my 'ead; an' the music comin' to me, an' the cheers an cannon, till I got almost a hanarchist an' wanted to blow out the brains o' the Lord Chamberlain.'

Why the Lord Chamberlain I could not precisely see, nor could he, but that was the way he felt, he said conclusively, and there was no more discussion.

As night drew on, the city became a blaze of light. Splashes of colour, green, amber, and ruby, caught the eye at every point, and 'E.R.', in great cut-crystal letters and backed by flaming gas, was everywhere. The crowds in the streets increased by hundreds of thousands, and though the police sternly put down mafficking, drunkenness and rough play abounded. The tired workers seemed to have gone mad with the relaxation and excitement, and they surged and danced down the streets, men and women, old and young, with linked arms and in long rows, singing, 'I may be crazy, but I love you', 'Dolly Gray', and 'The Honeysuckle and the Bee' – the last rendered something like this:

> 'Yew aw the enn, ennyseckle, Oi em ther bee,
> Oi'd like ter sip ther enny from those red lips, yew see.'

I sat on a bench on the Thames Embankment, looking across the illuminated water. It was approaching midnight, and before me poured the better class of merrymakers, shunning the more riotous streets and returning home. On the bench beside me sat two ragged creatures, a man and a woman, nodding and dozing. The woman sat with her arms clasped across the breast, holding tightly, her body in constant play – now dropping forward till it seemed its balance would be overcome and she would fall to the pavement; now inclining to the left, sideways, till her head rested on the man's shoulder; and now to the right, stretched and strained, till the pain of it awoke her and she sat bolt upright. Whereupon the dropping forward would begin again and go through its cycle till she was aroused by the strain and stretch.

Every little while boys and young men stopped long enough to go behind the bench and give vent to sudden and fiendish shouts. This always jerked the man and woman abruptly from their sleep; and at sight of the startled woe upon their faces the crowd would roar with laughter as it flooded past.

This was the most striking thing, the general heartlessness exhibited on every hand. It is a commonplace, the homeless on the benches, the poor miserable folk who may be teased and are harmless. Fifty thousand people must have passed the bench while I sat upon it, and not one, on such a jubilee occasion as the crowning of the King, felt his heart-strings touched sufficiently to come up and say to the woman: 'Here's sixpence; go and get a bed.' But the women, especially the young women, made witty remarks upon the woman nodding, and invariably set their companions laughing.

To use a Briticism, it was 'cruel'; the corresponding Americanism was more appropriate – it was 'fierce'. I confess I began to grow incensed at this happy crowd streaming by, and to extract a sort of satisfaction from the London statistics which demonstrate that one in every four adults is destined to die on public charity, either in the workhouse, the infirmary, or the asylum.

I talked with the man. He was fifty-four and a broken-down docker. He could only find odd work when there was a large demand for labour, for the younger and stronger men were preferred when times were slack. He had spent a week, now, on the benches of the Embankment; but things looked brighter for next week, and he might possibly get in a few days' work and have a bed in some doss-house. He had lived all his life in London, save for five years, when, in 1878, he saw foreign service in India.

Of course he would eat; so would the girl. Days like this were uncommon hard on such as they, though the coppers were so busy poor folk could get in more sleep. I awoke the girl, or woman, rather, for she was 'Eyght an' twenty, sir', and we started for a coffee-house.

'Wot a lot o' work puttin' up the lights,' said the man at sight of some building superbly illuminated. This was the keynote of his being. All his life he had worked, and the whole objective universe, as well as his own soul, he could express in terms only of work. 'Coronations is some good,' he went on. 'They give work to men.'

'But your belly is empty,' I said.

'Yes,' he answered. 'I tried, but there wasn't any chawnce. My age is against me. Wot do you work at? Seafarin' chap, eh? I knew it from yer clothes.'

'I know wot you are,' said the girl, 'an Eyetalian.'

'No 'e ayn't,' the man cried heatedly. ' 'E's a Yank, that's wot 'e is. I know.'

'Lord, lumme, look a' that,' she exclaimed, as we debouched upon the Strand, choked with the roaring, reeling Coronation crowd, the men bellowing and the girls singing in high throaty notes:

> 'Oh! on Coronation D'y, on Coronation D'y,
> We'll 'ave a spree, a jubilee, an' shout 'Ip, 'ip, 'ooray;
> For we'll all be merry, drinkin' whisky, wine, and sherry
> We'll all be merry on Coronation D'y.'

' 'Ow dirty I am, bein' around the w'y I 'ave,' the woman said, as she sat down in a coffee-house, wiping the sleep and grime from the corners of her eyes. 'An' the sights I 'ave seen this d'y, an' I enjoyed it, though it was lonesome by myself. An' the duchesses an' the lydies 'ad sich gran' white dresses. They was jest bu'ful, bu'ful.'

'I'm Irish,' she said, in answer to a question. 'My nyme's Eyethorne.'

'What?' I asked.

'Eyethorne, sir; Eyethorne.'

'Spell it.'

'H-a-y-t-h-o-r-n-e, Eyethorne.'

'Oh,' I said, 'Irish Cockney.'

'Yes, sir. London-born.'

She had lived happily at home till her father died, killed in an accident, when she had found herself on the world. One brother was in the army, and the other brother, engaged in keeping a wife and eight children on twenty shillings a week and unsteady employment, could do nothing for her. She had been out of London once in her life, to a place in Essex, twelve miles away, where she had picked fruit for three weeks: 'An' I was as brown as a berry w'en I come back. You won't b'lieve it, but I was.'

The last place in which she had worked was a coffee-house, hours from seven in the morning till eleven at night, and for which she had received five shillings a week and her food. Then she had fallen sick, and since emerging from the hospital had been unable to find anything to do. She wasn't feeling up to much, and the last two nights had been spent in the street.

Between them they stowed away a prodigious amount of food, this man and woman, and it was not till I had duplicated and triplicated their original orders that they showed signs of easing down.

Once she reached across and felt the texture of my coat and shirt, and remarked upon the good clothes the Yanks wore. My rags good clothes! It put me to the blush; but, on inspecting them more closely and on examining the clothes worn by the man and woman, I began to feel quite well dressed and respectable.

'What do you expect to do in the end?' I asked them. 'You know you're growing older every day.'

'Work'ouse,' said he.

'Gawd blimey if I do,' said she. 'There's no 'ope for me, I know, but I'll die on the streets. No work'ouse for me, thank you. No indeed,' she sniffed in the silence that fell.

'After you have been out all night in the streets,' I asked, 'What do you do in the morning for something to eat?'

'Try to get a penny, if you 'aven't one saved over,' the man explained. 'Then go to a coffee-'ouse an' get a mug o' tea.'

'But I don't see how that is to feed you,' I objected.

The pair smiled knowingly.

'You drink your tea in little sips,' he went on, 'making it last its longest. An' you look sharp, an' there's some as leaves a bit be'ind 'em'

'It's s'prisin', the food wot some people leaves,' the woman broke in.

'The thing,' said the man judicially, as the trick dawned upon me, 'is to get 'old o' the penny.'

As we started to leave, Miss Haythorne gathered up a couple of crusts from the neighbouring tables and thrust them somewhere into her rags.

66

'Cawn't wyste 'em, you know,' said she; to which the docker nodded, tucking away a couple of crusts himself.

At three in the morning I strolled up the Embankment. It was a gala night for the homeless, for the police were elsewhere; and each bench was jammed with sleeping occupants. There were as many women as men, and the great majority of them, male and female, were old. Occasionally a boy was to be seen. On one bench I noticed a family, a man sitting upright with a sleeping babe in his arms, his wife asleep, her head on his shoulder, and in her lap the head of a sleeping youngster. The man's eyes were wide open. He was staring out over the water and thinking, which is not a good thing for a shelterless man with a family to do. It would not be a pleasant thing to speculate upon his thoughts; but this I know, and all London knows, that the cases of out-of-works killing their wives and babies is not an uncommon happening.

One cannot walk along the Thames Embankment, in the small hours of morning, from the Houses of Parliament, past Cleopatra's Needle, to Waterloo Bridge, without being reminded of the sufferings, seven and twenty centuries old, recited by the author of 'Job':

There are that remove the landmarks; they violently take away flocks and feed them.

They drive away the ass of the fatherless, they take the widow's ox for a pledge.

They turn the needy out of the way; the poor of the earth hide themselves together.

Behold, as wild asses in the desert they go forth to their work, seeking diligently for meat; the wilderness yieldeth them food for their children.

They cut their provender in the field, and they glean the vintage of the wicked.

They lie all night naked without clothing, and have no covering in the cold.

They are wet with the showers of the mountains, and embrace the rock for want of shelter.

There are that pluck the fatherless from the breast, and take a pledge of the poor.

So that they go about naked without clothing, and being an hungered they carry the sheaves. – Job xxiv, vv. 2–10.

Seven and twenty centuries agone! And it is all as true and apposite today in the innermost centre of this Christian civilization whereof Edward VII is king.

CHAPTER THIRTEEN

DAN CULLEN, DOCKER

I STOOD, yesterday, in a room in one of the 'Municipal Dwellings', not far from Leman Street. If I looked into a dreary future and saw that I would have to live in such a room until I died, I should immediately go down, plump into the Thames, and cut the tenancy short.

It was not a room. Courtesy to the language will no more permit it to be called a room than it will permit a hovel to be called a mansion. It was a den, a lair. Seven feet by eight were its dimensions, and the ceiling was so low as not to give the cubic air space required by a British soldier in barracks. A crazy couch, with ragged coverlets, occupied nearly half the room. A rickety table, a chair and a couple of boxes left little space in which to turn around. Five dollars would have purchased everything in sight. The floor was bare, while the walls and ceiling were literally covered with blood marks and splotches. Each mark represented a violent death – of an insect, for the place swarmed with vermin, a plague with which no person could cope single-handed.

The man who had occupied this hole, one Dan Cullen, docker, was dying in hospital. Yet he had impressed his personality on his miserable surroundings sufficiently to give an inkling as to what sort of man he was. On the walls were cheap pictures of Garibaldi, Engels, Dan Burns, and other labour leaders, while on the table lay one of Walter Besant's novels. He knew his Shakespeare, I was told, and had read history, sociology, and economics. And he was self-educated.

On the table, amidst a wonderful disarray, lay a sheet of paper on which was scrawled: *Mr. Cullen, please return the large white jug and corkscrew I lent you* – articles loaned, during the first stages of his sickness, by a woman neighbour, and demanded back in anticipation of his death. A large white jug and a corkscrew are far too valuable to a creature of the Abyss to permit another creature to die in peace. To the last, Dan Cullen's soul must be harrowed by the sordidness out of which it strove vainly to rise.

It is a brief little story, the story of Dan Cullen, but there is much to read between the lines. He was born lowly, in a city and land where the lines of caste are tightly drawn. All his days he toiled hard with his body; and because he had opened the books, and been caught up by the fires of the spirit, and could 'write a letter like a lawyer', he had been selected by his fellows to toil hard for them with his brain. He became a leader of the fruit-porters, represented the dockers on the London Trades Council, and wrote trenchant articles for the labour journals.

He did not cringe to other men, even though they were his economic masters, and controlled the means whereby he lived, and he spoke his mind freely, and fought the good fight. In the 'Great Dock Strike' he was guilty of taking a leading part. And that was the end of Dan Cullen. From that day he was a marked man, and every day, for ten years and more, he was 'paid off' for what he had done.

A docker is a casual labourer. Work ebbs and flows, and he works or does not work according to the amount of goods on hand to be moved. Dan Cullen was discriminated against. While he was not absolutely turned away (which would have caused trouble, and

68

which would certainly have been more merciful), he was called in by the foreman to do not more than two or three days' work per week. This is what is called being 'disciplined', or 'drilled'. It means being starved. There is no politer word. Ten years of it broke his heart, and broken-hearted men cannot live.

He took to his bed in his terrible den, which grew more terrible with his helplessness. He was without kith or kin, a lonely old man, embittered and pessimistic, fighting vermin the while and looking at Garibaldi, Engels, and Dan Burns gazing down at him from the blood-bespattered walls. No one came to see him in that crowded municipal barracks (he had made friends with none of them), and he was left to rot.

But from the far reaches of the East End came a cobbler and his son, his sole friends. They cleansed his room, brought fresh linen from home, and took from off his limbs the sheets, greyish-black with dirt. And they brought to him one of the Queen's Bounty nurses from Aldgate.

She washed his face, shook up his couch, and talked with him. It was interesting to talk with him – until he learned her name. Oh, yes, Blank was her name, she replied innocently, and Sir George Blank was her brother. Sir George Blank, eh? thundered old Dan Cullen on his death-bed; Sir George Blank, solicitor to the docks at Cardiff, who, more than any other man, had broken up the Dockers' Union of Cardiff, and was knighted? And she was his sister? Thereupon Dan Cullen sat up on his crazy couch and pronounced anathema upon her and all her breed; and she fled, to return no more, strongly impressed with the ungratefulness of the poor.

Dan Cullen's feet became swollen with dropsy. He sat up all day on the side of the bed (to keep the water out of his body), no mat on the floor, a thin blanket on his legs, and an old coat around his shoulders. A missionary brought him a pair of paper slippers, worth fourpence (I saw them), and proceeded to offer up fifty prayers or so for the good of Dan Cullen's soul. But Dan Cullen was the sort of man that wanted his soul left alone. He did not care to have Tom, Dick, or Harry, on the strength of fourpenny slippers, tampering with it. He asked the missionary kindly to open the window, so that he might toss the slippers out. And the missionary went away, to return no more, likewise impressed with the ungratefulness of the poor.

The cobbler, a brave old hero himself, though unaneled and unsung, went privily to the head office of the big fruit brokers for whom Dan Cullen had worked as a casual labourer for thirty years. Their system was such that the work was almost entirely done by casual hands. The cobbler told them the man's desperate plight, old, broken, dying, without help or money, reminded them that he had worked for them thirty years, and asked them to do something for him.

'Oh,' said the manager, remembering Dan Cullen without having to refer to the books, 'you see, we make it a rule never to help casuals, and we can do nothing.'

Nor did they do anything, not even sign a letter asking for Dan Cullen's admission to a hospital. And it is not so easy to get into a hospital in London Town. At Hampstead, if he passed the doctors, at least four months would elapse before he could get in, there were so many on the books ahead of him. The cobbler finally got him into the Whitechapel Infirmary, where he visited him frequently. Here he found that Dan Cullen had succumbed to the prevalent feeling, that, being hopeless, they were hurrying him out of the way. A fair and logical conclusion, one must agree, for an old and broken man to arrive at, who has been resolutely 'disciplined' and 'drilled' for ten years. When they sweated him for Bright's disease to remove the fat from the kidneys, Dan Cullen contended that the sweating was hastening his death; while Bright's disease, being a wasting away of the kidneys, there was therefore no fat to remove, and the doctor's excuse was a palpable lie. Whereupon the doctor became wroth, and did not come near him for nine days.

Then his bed was tilted up so that his feet and legs were elevated. At once dropsy appeared in the body, and Dan Cullen contended that the thing was done in order to run the water down into his body from his legs and kill him more quickly. He demanded his discharge, though they told him he would die on the stairs, and dragged himself, more dead than alive to the cobbler's shop. At the moment of writing this, he is dying at the Temperance Hospital, into which his staunch friend, the cobbler, moved heaven and earth to have him admitted.

Poor Dan Cullen! A Jude the Obscure, who reached out after knowledge, who toiled with his body in the day and studied in the watches of the night; who dreamed his dream and struck valiantly for the Cause; a patriot, a lover of human freedom, and a fighter unafraid; and in the end, not gigantic enough to beat down the conditions which baffled and stifled him, a cynic and a pessimist, gasping his final agony on a pauper's couch in a charity ward – 'For a man to die who might have been wise and was not, this I call a tragedy.'

CHAPTER FOURTEEN

HOPS AND HOPPERS

So far has the divorcement of the worker from the soil proceeded, that the farming districts, the civilized world over, are dependent upon the cities for the gathering of the harvests. Then it is, when the land is spilling its ripe wealth to waste, that the street folk, who have been driven away from the soil, are called back to it again. But in England they return, not as prodigals, but as outcasts still, as vagrants and pariahs, to be doubted and flouted by their country brethren, to sleep in gaols and casual wards, or under the hedges, and to live the Lord knows how.

It is estimated that Kent alone requires eighty thousand of the street people to pick her hops. And out they come, obedient to the call, which is the call of their bellies and of the lingering dregs of adventure-lust still in them. Slum, stews and ghetto pour them forth, and the festering contents of slum, stews, and ghetto are undiminished. Yet they overrun the country like an army of ghouls, and the country does not want them. They are out of place. As they drag their squat, misshapen bodies along the highways and byways, they resemble some vile spawn from underground. Their very presence, the fact of their existence, is an outrage to the fresh, bright sun and the green and growing things. The clean, upstanding trees cry shame upon them and their withered crookedness, and their rottenness is a slimy desecration of the sweetness and purity of nature.

Is the picture overdrawn? It all depends. For one who sees and thinks life in terms of shares and coupons, it is certainly overdrawn. But for one who sees and thinks life in terms of manhood and womanhood, it cannot be overdrawn. Such hordes of beastly wretchedness and inarticulate misery are no compensation for a millionaire brewer who lives in a West End palace, sates himself with the sensuous delights of London's golden theatres, hobnobs with lordlings and princelings, and is knighted by the King. Wins his spurs – God forbid! In old time the great blond beasts rode in the battle's van and won their spurs by cleaving men from pate to chine. And, after all, it is finer to kill a strong man with a clean-slicing blow of singing steel than to make a beast of him, and of his seed through the generations, by the artful and spidery manipulation of industry and politics.

But to return to the hops. Here the divorcement from the soil is as apparent as in every other agricultural line in England. While the manufacture of beer steadily increases, the growth of hops steadily decreases. In 1835 the acreage under hops was 71,327. To-day it stands at 48,024, a decrease of 3,103 from the acreage of last year.

Small as the acreage is this year, a poor summer and terrible storms reduced the yield. This misfortune is divided between the people who own hops and the people who pick hops. The owners perforce must put up with less of the nicer things of life, the pickers with less grub, of which, in the best of times, they never get enough. For weary weeks headlines like the following have appeared in the London papers:

TRAMPS PLENTIFUL, BUT THE HOPS ARE FEW AND NOT
YET READY

Then there have been numberless paragraphs like this:
From the neighbourhood of the hop fields comes news of a distressing nature. The bright outburst of the last two days has sent many hundreds of hoppers into Kent, who will have to wait till the fields are ready for them. At Dover the number of vagrants in the workhouse is treble the number there last year at this time, and in other towns the lateness of the season is responsible for a large increase in the number of casuals.

To cap their wretchedness, when at last the picking had begun, hops and hoppers were well-nigh swept away by a frightful storm of wind, rain, and hail. The hops were stripped clean from the poles and pounded into the earth, while the hoppers, seeking shelter from the stinging hail, were close to drowning in their huts and camps on the low-lying ground. Their condition after the storm was pitiable, their state of vagrancy more pronounced than ever; for, poor crop that it was, its destruction had taken away the chance of earning a few pennies, and nothing remained for thousands of them but to 'pad the hoof' back to London.

'We ayn't crossin'-sweepers,' they said, turning away from the ground, carpeted ankle-deep with hops.

Those that remained grumbled savagely among the half-stripped poles at the seven bushels for a shilling – a rate paid in good seasons when the hops are in prime condition, and a rate likewise paid in bad seasons by the growers because they cannot afford more.

I passed through Teston and East and West Farleigh shortly after the storm, and listened to the grumbling of the hoppers and saw the hops rotting on the ground. At the hothouses of Barham Court, thirty thousand panes of glass had been broken by the hail, while peaches, plums, pears, apples, rhubarb, cabbages, mangolds, everything, had been pounded to pieces and torn to shreds.

All of which was too bad for the owners, certainly; but at the worst, not one of them, for one meal, would have to go short of food or drink. Yet it was to them that the newspapers devoted columns of sympathy, their pecuniary losses being detailed at harrowing length. 'Mr. Herbert L— calculates his loss at £8,000'; 'Mr. F—, of brewery fame, who rents all the land in this parish, loses £10,000'; and 'Mr. L—, the Wateringbury brewer, brother to Mr. Herbert L—, is another heavy loser.' As for the hoppers, they did not count. Yet I venture to assert that the several almost-square meals lost by the underfed William Buggles, and underfed Mrs. Buggles, and the underfed Buggles kiddies, was a greater tragedy than the £10,000 lost by Mr. F—. And, in addition, underfed William Buggles' tragedy might be multiplied by thousands where Mr. F—'s could not be multiplied by five.

To see how William Buggles and his kind fared, I donned my seafaring togs and started out to get a job. With me was a young East London cobbler, Bert, who had yielded to the lure of adventure and joined me for the trip. Acting on my advice, he had brought his 'worst rags', and as we hiked up the London road out of Maidstone he was worrying greatly for fear we had come too ill-dressed for the business.

Nor was he to be blamed. When we stopped in a tavern the publican eyed us gingerly, nor did his demeanour brighten till we showed him the colour of our cash. The natives along the coast were all dubious; and 'beanfeasters' from London, dashing past in coaches, cheered and jeered and shouted insulting things after us. But before we were done with the Maidstone district my friend found that we were as well clad, if not better, than the average hopper. Some of the bunches of rags we chanced upon were marvellous.

'The tide is out,' called a gypsy-looking woman to her mates, as we came up a long row of bins into which the pickers were stripping the hops.

'Do you twig?' Bert whispered. 'She's on to you.'

I twigged. And it must be confessed the figure was an apt one. When the tide is out boats are left on the beach and do not sail, and a sailor, when the tide is out, does not sail either. My seafaring togs and my presence in the hop field proclaimed that I was a seaman without a ship, a man on the beach, and very like a craft at low water.

'Can yer give us a job, governor?' Bert asked the bailiff, a kindly faced and elderly man who was very busy.

His 'No' was decisively uttered; but Bert clung on and followed him about, and I followed after, pretty well all over the field. Whether our persistency struck the bailiff as anxiety to work, or whether he was affected by our hard-luck appearance and tale, neither Bert nor I succeeded in making out; but in the end he softened his heart and found us the one unoccupied bin in the place – a bin deserted by two other men, from what I could learn, because of inability to make living wages.

'No bad conduct, mind ye,' warned the bailiff, as he left us at work in the midst of the women.

It was Saturday afternoon, and we knew quitting time would come early; so we applied ourselves earnestly to the task, desiring to learn if we could at least make our salt. It was simple work, woman's work, in fact, and not man's. We sat on the edge of the bin, between the standing hops, while a pole-puller supplied us with great fragrant branches. In an hour's time we became as expert as it is possible to become. As soon as the fingers became accustomed automatically to differentiate between hops and leaves and to strip half-a-dozen blossoms at a time there was no more to learn.

We worked nimbly, and as fast as the women themselves, though their bins filled more rapidly because of their swarming children, each of which picked with two hands almost as fast as we picked.

'Don'tcher pick too clean, it's against the rules,' one of the women informed us; and we took the tip and were grateful.

As the afternoon wore along, we realized that living wages could not be made – by men. Women could pick as much as men, and children could do almost as well as women; so it was impossible for a man to compete with a woman and half-a-dozen children; for it is the woman and half-a-dozen children who count as a unit, and by their combined capacity determine the unit's pay.

'I say, matey, I'm beastly hungry,' said I to Bert. We had not had any dinner.

'Blimey, but I could eat the 'ops,' he replied.

Whereupon we both lamented our negligence in not rearing up a numerous progeny to help us in this day of need. And in such fashion we whiled away the time and talked for the edification of

73

our neighbours. We quite won the sympathy of the pole-puller, a young country yokel, who now and again, emptied a few picked blossoms into our bin, it being part of his business to gather up the stray clusters torn off in the process of pulling.

With him we discussed how much we could 'sub', and were informed that while we were being paid a shilling for seven bushels, we could only 'sub', or have advanced to us, a shilling for every twelve bushels. Which is to say that the pay for five out of every twelve bushels was withheld – a method of the growers to hold the hopper to his work whether the crop runs good or bad, and especially if it runs bad.

After all, it was pleasant sitting there in the bright sunshine, the golden pollen showering from our hands, the pungent aromatic odour of the hops biting our nostrils, and the while remembering dimly the sounding cities whence these people came. Poor street people! Poor gutter folk! Even they grow earth-hungry, and yearn vaguely for the soil from which they have been driven, and for the free life in the open, and the wind and rain and sun all undefiled by city smirches. As the sea calls to the sailor, so calls the land to them; and, deep down in their aborted and decaying carcasses, they are stirred strangely by the peasant memories of their forebears who lived before cities were. And in incomprehensible ways they are made glad by the earth smells and sights and sounds which their blood has not forgotten though unremembered by them.

'No more 'ops, matey,' Bert complained.

It was five o'clock, and the pole-pullers had knocked off, so that everything could be cleaned up, there being no work on Sunday. For an hour we were forced idly to wait the coming of the measurers, our feet tingling with the frost which came on the heels of the setting sun. In the adjoining bin, two women and half-a-dozen children had picked nine bushels: so that the five bushels the measurers found in our bin demonstrated that we had done equally well, for the half-dozen children had ranged from nine to fourteen years of age.

Five bushels! We worked it out to eightpence ha'penny, or seventeen cents, for two men working three hours and a half. Fourpence farthing apiece! a little over a penny an hour! But we were allowed only to 'sub' fivepence of the total sum, though the tallykeeper, short of change, gave us sixpence. Entreaty was in vain. A hard-luck story could not move him. He proclaimed loudly that we had received a penny more than our due, and went his way.

Granting, for the sake of the argument, that we were what we represented ourselves to be – namely, poor men and broke – then here was our position: night was coming on; we had had no supper, much less dinner; and we possessed sixpence between us. I was hungry enough to eat three sixpenn'orths of food, and so was Bert. One thing was patent. By doing 16⅔ per cent justice to our stomachs, we would expend the sixpence, and our stomachs would still be gnawing under 83⅓ per cent injustice. Being broke again, we could sleep under a hedge, which was not so bad, though the cold would

74

sap an undue portion of what we had eaten. But the morrow was Sunday, on which we could do no work, though our silly stomachs would not knock off on that account. Here, then, was the problem: how to get three meals on Sunday, and two on Monday (for we could not make another 'sub' till Monday evening). We knew that the casual wards were overcrowded; also, that if we begged from farmer or villager, there was a large likelihood of our going to gaol for fourteen days. What was to be done? We looked at each other in despair –

– Not a bit of it. We joyfully thanked God that we were not as other men, especially hoppers, and went down the road to Maidstone, jingling in our pockets the half-crowns and florins we had brought from London.

CHAPTER FIFTEEN

THE SEA WIFE

You might not expect to find the Sea Wife in the heart of Kent, but that is where I found her, in a mean street, in the poor quarter of Maidstone. In her window she had no sign of lodgings to let, and persuasion was necessary before she could bring herself to let me sleep in her front room. In the evening I descended to the semi-subterranean kitchen, and talked with her and her old man, Thomas Mugridge by name.

And as I talked to them, all the subtleties and complexities of this tremendous machine civilization vanished away. It seemed that I went down through the skin and the flesh to the naked soul of it, and in Thomas Mugridge and his old woman gripped hold of the essence of this remarkable English breed. I found there the spirit of the wanderlust which has lured Albion's sons across the zones; and I found there the colossal unreckoning which has tricked the English into foolish squabblings and preposterous fights, and the doggedness and stubbornness which have brought them blindly through to empire and greatness; and likewise I found that vast, incomprehensible patience which has enabled the home population to endure under the burden of it all, to toil without complaint through the weary years, and docilely to yield the best of its sons to fight and colonize to the ends of the earth.

Thomas Mugridge was seventy-one years old and a little man. It was because he was little that he had not gone for a soldier. He had remained at home and worked. His first recollections were connected with work. He knew nothing else but work. He had worked all his days, and at seventy-one he still worked. Each morning saw him up with the lark and afield, a day labourer, for as such he had been born. Mrs. Mugridge was seventy-three. From seven years of age she had worked in the fields, doing a boy's work at first, and later a man's. She still worked, keeping the house shining, washing, boiling, and baking, and, with my advent, cooking for me and shaming

75

me by making my bed. At the end of threescore years and more of work they possessed nothing, had nothing to look forward to save more work. And they were contented. They expected nothing else, desired nothing else.

They lived simply. Their wants were few – a pint of beer at the end of the day, sipped in the semi-subterranean kitchen, a weekly paper to pore over for seven nights hand-running, and conversation as meditative and vacant as the chewing of a heifer's cud. From a wood engraving on the wall a slender angelic girl looked down upon them, and underneath was the legend: 'Our Future Queen'. And from a highly coloured lithograph alongside looked down a stout and elderly lady, with underneath: 'Our Queen – Diamond Jubilee'.

'What you earn is sweetest,' quoth Mrs. Mugridge, when I suggested that it was about time they took a rest.

'No, an' we don't want help,' said Thomas Mugridge, in reply to my question as to whether the children lent them a hand.

'We'll work till we dry up and blow away, mother an' me,' he added; and Mrs. Mugridge nodded her head in vigorous endorsement.

Fifteen children she had borne, and all were away and gone, or dead. The 'baby' however, lived in Maidstone, and she was twenty-seven. When the children married they had their hands full with their own families and troubles, like their fathers and mothers before them.

Where were the children? Ah, where were they not? Lizzie was in Australia; Mary was in Buenos Ayres; Poll was in New York; Joe had died in India – and so they called them up, the living and the dead, soldier and sailor, and colonist's wife, for the traveller's sake who sat in their kitchen.

They passed me a photograph. A trim young fellow in soldier's garb looked out at me.

'And which son is this?' I asked.

They laughed a hearty chorus. Son! Nay, grandson, just back from Indian service and a soldier-trumpeter to the King. His brother was in the same regiment with him. And so it ran, sons and daughters, and grandsons and daughters, world-wanderers and empire-builders, all of them, while the old folks stayed at home and worked at building empire too.

> 'There dwells a wife by the Northern Gate,
>   And a wealthy wife is she;
> She breeds a breed o' rovin' men
>   And casts them over sea.

> 'And some are drowned in deep water,
>   And some in sight of shore;
> And word goes back to the wary wife,
>   And ever she sends more.'

But the Sea Wife's child-bearing is about done. The stock is running out, and the planet is filling up. The wives of her sons may carry on the breed, but her work is past. The erstwhile men of

76

England are now the men of Australia, of Africa, of America. England has sent forth 'the best she breeds' for so long, and has destroyed those that remained so fiercely, that little remains for her to do but to sit down through the long nights and gaze at royalty on the wall.

The true British merchant seaman has passed away. The merchant service is no longer a recruiting ground for such sea dogs as fought with Nelson at Trafalgar and the Nile. Foreigners largely man the merchant ships, though Englishmen still continue to officer them and to prefer foreigners for'ard. In South Africa the colonial teaches the islander how to shoot, and the officers muddle and blunder; while at home the street people play hysterically at mafficking, and the War Office lowers the stature for enlistment.

It could not be otherwise. The most complacent Britisher cannot hope to draw off the life-blood, and underfeed, and keep it up forever. The average Mrs. Thomas Mugridge has been driven into the city, and she is not breeding very much of anything save an anaemic and sickly progeny which cannot find enough to eat. The strength of the English-speaking race today is not in the tight little island, but in the New World overseas, where are the sons and daughters of Mrs. Thomas Mugridge. The Sea Wife by the Northern Gate has just about done her work in the world, though she does not realize it. She must sit down and rest her tired loins for a space; and if the casual ward and the workhouse do not await her, it is because of the sons and daughters she has reared up against the day of her feebleness and decay.

CHAPTER SIXTEEN

PROPERTY v. PERSONS

IN a civilization frankly materialistic and based upon property, not soul, it is inevitable that property shall be exalted over soul, that crimes against property shall be considered far more serious than crimes against the person. To pound one's wife to a jelly and break a few of her ribs is a trivial offence compared with sleeping out under the naked stars because one has not the price of a doss. The lad who steals a few pears from a wealthy railway corporation is a greater menace to society than the young brute who commits an unprovoked assault upon an old man over seventy years of age. While the young girl who takes a lodging under the pretence that she has work commits so dangerous an offence, that, were she not severely punished, she and her kind might bring the whole fabric of property clattering to the ground. Had she unholily tramped Piccadilly and the Strand after midnight, the police would not have interfered with her, and she would have been able to pay for her lodging.

The following illustrative cases are culled from the police-court reports for a single week:

Widnes Police Court. Before Aldermen Gossage and Neil. Thomas Lynch, charged with being drunk and disorderly and with assaulting a constable. Defendant rescued a woman from custody, kicked the constable, and threw stones at him. Fined 3s. 6d. for the first offence, and 10s. and costs for the assault.

Glasgow Queen's Park Police Court. Before Bailie Norman Thompson. John Kane pleaded guilty to assaulting his wife. There were five previous convictions. Fined £2 2s.

Taunton County Petty Sessions. John Painter, a big, burly fellow, described as a labourer, charged with assaulting his wife. The woman received two severe black eyes, and her face was badly swollen. Fined £1 8s., including costs, and bound over to keep the peace.

Widnes Police Court Richard Bestwick and George Hunt, charged with trespassing in search of game. Hunt fined £1 and costs, Bestwick £2 and costs; in default, one month.

Shaftesbury Police Court. Before the Mayor (Mr. A. T. Carpenter). Thomas Baker, charged with sleeping out. Fourteen days.

Glasgow Central Police Court. Before Bailie Dunlop. Edward Morrison, a lad, convicted of stealing fifteen pears from a lorry at the railroad station. Seven days.

Doncaster Borough Police Court. Before Alderman Clark and other magistrates. James M'Gowan, charged under the Poaching Prevention Act with being found in possession of poaching implements and a number of rabbits. Fined £2 and costs, or one month.

Dunfermline Sheriff Court. Before Sheriff Gillespie. John Young, a pit-head worker, pleaded guilty to assaulting Alexander Storrar by beating him about the head and body with his fists, throwing him on the ground, and also striking him with a pit prop. Fined £1.

Kirkcaldy Police Court. Before Bailie Dishart. Simon Walker pleaded guilty to assaulting a man by striking and knocking him down. It was an unprovoked assault, and the magistrates described the accused as a perfect danger to the community. Fined 30s.

Mansfield Police Court. Before the Mayor, Messrs. F. J. Turner, J. Whitaker, F. Tidsbury, E. Holmes, and Dr. R. Nesbitt. Joseph Jackson, charged with assaulting Charles Nunn. Without any provocation, defendant struck the complainant a violent blow in the face, knocking him down, and then kicked him on the side of the head. He was rendered unconscious, and he remained under medical treatment for a fortnight. Fined 21s.

Perth Sheriff Court. Before Sheriff Sym. David Mitchell, charged with poaching. There were two previous convictions, the last being three years ago. The sheriff was asked to deal leniently with Mitchell, who was sixty-two years of age, and who offered no resistance to the gamekeeper. Four months.

Dundee Sheriff Court. Before Hon. Sheriff-Substitute R. C. Walker. John Murray, Donald Craig, and James Parkes, charged with poaching. Craig and Parkes fined £1 each or fourteen days; Murray, £5 or one month.

Reading Borough Police Court. Before Messrs. W. B. Monck, F. B. Parfitt, H. M. Wallis, and G. Gillagan, Alfred Masters, aged sixteen, charged with sleeping out on a waste piece of ground and having no visible means of subsistence. Seven days.

Salisbury City Petty Sessions. Before the Mayor, Messrs. C. Hoskins, G. Fullford, E. Alexander, and W. Marlow. James Moore, charged with stealing a pair of boots from outside a shop. Twenty-one days.

Horncastle Police Court. Before the Rev. W. P. Massingberd, the Rev. J. Graham, and Mr. N. Lucas Calcraft. George Brackenbury, a young labourer, convicted of what the magistrates characterized as an altogether unprovoked and brutal assault upon James Sargeant Foster, a man over seventy years of age. Fined £1 and 5s. 6d. costs.

Worksop Petty Sessions. Before Messrs. F. J. S. Foljambe, R. Eddison, and S. Smith. John Priestley, charged with assaulting the Rev. Leslie Graham. Defendant, who was drunk, was wheeling a perambulator and pushed it in front of a lorry, with the result that the perambulator was overturned and the baby in it thrown out. The lorry passed over the perambulator, but the baby was uninjured. Defendant then attacked the driver of the lorry, and afterwards assaulted the complainant, who remonstrated with him upon his conduct. In consequence of the injuries defendant inflicted, complainant had to consult a doctor. Fined 40s. and costs.

Rotherham West Riding Police Court. Before Messrs. C. Wright and G. Push and Colonel Stoddart. Benjamin Storey, Thomas Brammer, and Samuel Wilcock, charged with poaching. One month each.

Southampton County Police Court. Before Admiral J. C. Rowley, Mr. H. H. Culme-Seymour, and other magistrates. Henry Thorrington, charged with sleeping out. Seven days.

Eckington Police Court. Before Major L. B. Bowden, Messrs. R. Eyre, and H. A. Fowler, and Dr. Court. Joseph Watts, charged with stealing nine ferns from a garden. One month.

Ripley Petty Sessions. Before Messrs. J. B. Wheeler, W. D. Bembridge, and M. Hooper. Vincent Allen and George Hall, charged under the Poaching Prevention Act with being found in possession of a number of rabbits, and John Sparham, charged with aiding and abetting them. Hall and Sparham fined £1 17s. 4d., and Allen £2 17s. 4d., including costs; the former committed for fourteen days and the latter for one month in default of payment.

South-western Police Court, London. Before Mr. Rose. John Probyn, charged with doing grievous bodily harm to a constable. Prisoner had been kicking his wife, and also assaulting another woman who protested against his brutality. The constable tried to persuade him to go inside his house, but prisoner suddenly turned upon him, knocking him down by a blow on the face, kicking him as he lay on the ground, and attempting to strangle him. Finally the prisoner deliberately kicked the officer in a dangerous part, inflicting an injury which will keep him off duty for a long time to come. Six weeks.

Lambeth Police Court, London. Before Mr. Hopkins. 'Baby' Stuart aged nineteen, decribed as a chorus girl, charged with obtaining food and lodging to the value of 5s. by false pretences, and with intent to defraud Emma Brasier. Emma Brasier, complainant, lodging-house keeper of Atwell Road. Prisoner took apartments at her house on the representation that she was employed at the Crown Theatre. After prisoner had been in her house two or three days, Mrs. Brasier made inquiries, and, finding the girl's story untrue, gave her into custody. Prisoner told the magistrate that she would have worked had she not had such bad health. Six weeks' hard labour.

CHAPTER SEVENTEEN

INEFFICIENCY

I STOPPED a moment to listen to an argument on the Mile End Waste. It was night-time, and they were all workmen of the better class. They had surrounded one of their number, a pleasant-faced man of thirty, and were giving it to him rather heatedly.

'But 'ow about this 'ere cheap immigration?' one of them demanded. 'The Jews of Whitechapel, say, a-cutting our throats right along?'

'You can't blame them,' was the answer. 'They're just like us, and they've got to live. Don't blame the man who offers to work cheaper than you and gets your job.'

'But 'ow about the wife an' kiddies?' his interlocutor demanded.

'There you are,' came the answer. 'How about the wife and kiddies of the man who works cheaper than you and gets your job? Eh? How about his wife and kiddies? He's more interested in them than in yours, and he can't see them starve. So he cuts the price of labour and out you go. But you mustn't blame him, poor devil. He can't help it. Wages always come down when two men are after the same job. That's the fault of competition, not of the man who cuts the price.'

'But wyges don't come down when there's a union,' the objection was made.

'And there you are again, right on the head. The union checks competition among the labourers, but makes it harder where there are no unions. There's where your cheap labour of Whitechapel comes in. They're unskilled, and have no unions, and cut each other's throats, and ours in the bargain, if we don't belong to a strong union.'

Without going further into the argument, this man on the Mile End Waste pointed the moral that when two men were after the one job wages were bound to fall. Had he gone deeper into the matter, he would have found that even the union, say, twenty thousand strong, could not hold up wages if twenty thousand idle men were trying to displace the union men. This is admirably instanced, just now, by the return and disbandment of the soldiers from South Africa. They find themselves, by tens of thousands, in desperate straits in the army of the unemployed. There is a general decline in wages throughout the land, which, giving rise to labour disputes and strikes, is taken advantage of by the unemployed, who gladly pick up the tools thrown down by the strikers.

Sweating, starvation wages, armies of unemployed, and great numbers of the homeless and shelterless are inevitable when there are more men to do work than there is work for men to do. The men and women I have met upon the streets, and in the spikes and pegs, are not there because as a mode of life it may be considered a 'soft snap'. I have sufficiently outlined the hardships they undergo to demonstrate that their existence is anything but 'soft'.

It is a matter of sober calculation, here in England, that it is softer to work for twenty shillings a week, and have regular food, and a bed at night, than it is to walk the streets. The man who walks the streets suffers more, and works harder, for far less return. I have depicted the nights they spend, and how, driven in by physical exhaustion, they go to the casual ward for a 'rest up'. Nor is the casual ward a soft snap. To pick four pounds of oakum, break twelve hundred-weight of stones, or perform the most revolting tasks, in return for the miserable food and shelter they receive, is an unqualified extravagance on the part of the men who are guilty of it. On the part of the authorities it is sheer robbery. They give the men far less for their labour than do the capitalistic employers. The wage for the same amount of labour, performed for a private employer, would buy them better beds, bettter food, more good cheer, and, above all, greater freedom.

As I say, it is an extravagance for a man to patronize a casual ward. And that they know it themselves is shown by the way these men shun it till driven in by physical exhaustion. Then why do they do it? Not because they are discouraged workers. The very opposite is true; they are discouraged vagabonds. In the United States the tramp is almost invariably a discouraged worker. He finds tramping a softer mode of life than working. But this is not true in England. Here the powers that be do their utmost to discourage the tramp and vagabond, and he is, in all truth, a mightily discouraged creature. He knows that two shillings a day, which is only fifty cents, will buy him three fair meals, a bed at night, and leave him a couple of pennies for pocket money. He would rather work for these two shillings than for the charity of the casual ward; for he knows that he would not have to work so hard, and that he would not be so abominably treated. He does not do so, however, because there are more men to do work than there is work for men to do.

When there are more men than there is work to be done, a sifting-out process must obtain. In every branch of industry the less efficient are crowded out. Being crowded out because of inefficiency, they cannot go up, but must descend, and continue to descend, until they reach their proper level, a place in the industrial fabric where they are efficient. It follows, therefore, and it is inexorable, that the least efficient must descend to the very bottom, which is the shambles wherein they perish miserably.

A glance at the confirmed inefficients at the bottom demonstrates that they are, as a rule, mental, physical, and moral wrecks. The exceptions to the rule are the late arrivals, who are merely very inefficient, and upon whom the wrecking process is just beginning to operate. All the forces here, it must be remembered, are destructive. The good body (which is there because its brain is not quick and capable) is speedily wrenched and twisted out of shape; the clean mind (which is there because of its weak body) is speedily fouled and contaminated. The mortality is excessive, but, even then, they die far too lingering deaths.

Here, then, we have the the construction of the Abyss and the shambles. Throughout the whole industrial fabric a constant elimination is going on. The inefficient are weeded out and flung downward. Various things constitute inefficiency. The engineer who is irregular or irresponsible will sink down until he finds his place, say, as a casual labourer, an occupation irregular in its very nature and in which there is little or no responsibility. Those who are slow and clumsy, who suffer from weakness of body or mind, or lack nervous, mental, and physical stamina, must sink down, sometimes rapidly, sometimes step by step, to the bottom. Accident, by disabling an efficient worker, will make him inefficient, and down he must go. And the worker who becomes aged, with failing energy and numbing brain, must begin the frightful descent which knows no stopping-place short of the bottom and death.

In this last instance, the statistics of London tell a terrible tale. The population of London is one-seventh of the total population of the United Kingdom, and in London, year in and year out, one adult in every four dies on public charity, either in the workhouse, the hospital, or the asylum. When the fact that the well-to-do do not end thus is taken into consideration, it becomes manifest that it is the fate of at least one in every three adult workers to die on public charity.

As an illustration of how a good worker may suddenly become inefficient, and what then happens to him, I am tempted to give the case of M'Garry, a man thirty-two years of age, and an inmate of the workhouse. The extracts are quoted from the annual report of the trade union.

I worked at Sullivan's place in Widnes, better known as the British Alkali Chemical Works. I was working in a shed, and I had to cross the yard. It was ten o'clock at night, and there was no light about. While crossing the yard I felt something take hold of my leg and screw it off. I became unconscious; I didn't know what became of me for a day or two. On the following Sunday night I came to my senses, and found myself in the hospital. I asked the nurse what was to do with my legs, and she told me both legs were off.

There was a stationary crank in the yard, let into the ground; the hole was 18 inches long, 15 inches deep, and 15 inches wide. The crank revolved in the hole three revolutions a minute. There was no fence or covering over the hole. Since my accident they have stopped it altogether, and have covered the hole up with a piece of sheet iron. ... They gave me £25. They didn't reckon that as compensation; they said it was only for charity's sake. Out of that I paid £9 for a machine by which to wheel myself about.

I was labouring at the time I got my legs off. I got twenty-four shillings a week, rather better pay than the other men, because I used to take shifts. When there was heavy work to be done I used to be picked out to do it. Mr. Manton, the manager, visited me at the hospital several times. When I was getting better, I asked him if he would be able to find me a job. He told me not to trouble myself, as the firm was not cold-hearted. I would be right enough in any case. ... Mr. Manton stopped coming to see me; and the last time, he said he thought of asking the directors to give me a fifty-pound note, so I could go home to my friends in Ireland.

Poor M'Garry! He received rather better pay than the other men because he was ambitious and took shifts, and when heavy work was to be done he was the man picked out to do it. And then the thing happened, and he went into the workhouse. The alternative to the workhouse is to go home to Ireland and burden his friends for the rest of his life. Comment is superfluous.

It must be understood that inefficiency is not determined by the workers themselves, but is determined by the demand for labour. If three men seek one position, the most efficient man will get it. The other two, no matter how capable they may be, will none the less be inefficients. If Germany, Japan, and the United States should capture the entire world market for iron, coal, and textiles, at once the English workers would be thrown idle by hundreds of thousands. Some would emigrate, but the rest would rush their labour into the remaining industries. A general shaking up of the workers from top to bottom would result; and when equilibrium had been restored, the number of the inefficients at the bottom of the Abyss would have been increased by hundreds of thousands. On the other hand, conditions remaining constant and all the workers doubling their efficiency, there would still be as many inefficients, though each inefficient were twice as capable as he had been and more capable than many of the efficients had previously been.

When there are more men to work than there is work for men to do, just as many men as are in excess of work will be inefficients,

83

and as inefficients they are doomed to lingering and painful destruction. It shall be the aim of future chapters to show, by their work and manner of living, not only how the inefficients are weeded out and destroyed, but to show how inefficients are being constantly and wantonly created by the forces of industrial society as it exists today.

CHAPTER EIGHTEEN

WAGES

WHEN I learned that in Lesser London there were 1,292,737 people who received twenty-one shillings or less a week per family, I became interested as to how the wages could best be spent in order to maintain the physical efficiency of such families. Families of six, seven, eight or ten being beyond consideration, I have based the following table upon a family of five – a father, mother, and three children; while I have made twenty-one shillings equivalent to $5.25, though actually, twenty-one shillings are equivalent to about $5.11.

Rent	$1.50 or	6s.0d.
Bread	1.00 ,,	4s.0d.
Meat	0.87½ ,,	3s.6d.
Vegetables	0.62½ ,,	2s.6d.
Coals	0.25 ,,	1s.0d.
Tea	0.18 ,,	9d.
Oil	0.16 ,,	8d.
Sugar	0.18 ,,	9d.
Milk	0.12 ,,	6d.
Soap	0.08 ,,	4d.
Butter	0.20 ,,	10d.
Firewood	0.08 ,,	4d.
Total	$5.25	21s.2d.

An analysis of one item alone will show how little room there is for waste. *Bread*, $1 : for a family of five, for seven days, one dollar's worth of bread will give each a daily ration of 2 6/7ths cents; and if they eat three meals a day, each may consume per meal 9½ mills' worth of bread, a little less than one halfpennyworth. Now bread is the heaviest item. They will get less of meat per mouth each meal, and still less vegetables; while the smaller items become too microscopic for consideration. On the other hand, these food articles are all bought at small retail, the most expensive and wasteful method of purchasing.

While the table given above will permit no extravagance, no overloading of stomachs, it will be noticed that there is no surplus. The whole guinea is spent for food and rent. There is no pocket-money left over. Does the man buy a glass of beer, the family must eat that

84

much less; and in so far as it eats less, just that far will it impair its physical efficiency. The members of this family cannot ride in buses or trams, cannot write letters, take outings, go to a 'tu'penny gaff' for cheap vaudeville, join social or benefit clubs, nor can they buy sweetmeats, tobacco, books, or newspapers.

And further, should one child (and there are three) require a pair of shoes, the family must strike meat for a week from its bill of fare. And since there are five pairs of feet requiring shoes, and five heads requiring hats, and five bodies requiring clothes, and since there are laws regulating indecency, the family must constantly impair its physical efficiency in order to keep warm and out of gaol. For notice, when rent, coals, oil, soap, and firewood are extracted from the weekly income, there remains a daily allowance for food of 4½d. to each person; and that 4½d. cannot be lessened by buying clothes without impairing the physical efficiency.

All of which is hard enough. But the thing happens; the husband and father breaks his leg or his neck. No 4½d. a day per mouth for food is coming in; no halfpenny worth of bread per meal; and, at the end of the week, no six shillings for rent. So out they must go, to the streets or the workhouse, or to a miserable den, somewhere, in which the mother will desperately endeavour to hold the family together on the ten shillings she may possibly be able to earn.

While in London there are 1,292,737 people who receive twenty-one shillings or less a week per family, it must be remembered that we have investigated a family of five living on a twenty-one shilling basis. There are larger families, there are many familes that live on less than twenty-one shillings, and there is much irregular employment. The question naturally arises, How do *they* live? The answer is that they do not live. They do not know what life is. They drag out a subbestial existence until mercifully released by death.

Before descending to the fouler depths, let the case of the telephone girls be cited. Here are clean, fresh English maids, for whom a higher standard of living than that of the beasts is absolutely necessary. Otherwise they cannot remain clean, fresh English maids. On entering the service, a telephone girl receives a weekly wage of eleven shillings. If she be quick and clever, she may, at the end of five years attain a maximum wage of one pound. Recently a table of such a girl's weekly expenditure was furnished to Lord Londonderry. Here it is:

	s.	d.
Rent, fire, and light	7	6
Board at home	3	6
Board at the office	4	6
Street car fare	1	6
Laundry	1	0
Total	18	0

This leaves nothing for clothes, recreation or sickness. And yet many of the girls are receiving, not eighteen shillings, but eleven

85

shillings, twelve shillings, and fourteen shillings per week. They must have clothes and recreation, and –

> Man to Man so oft unjust,
> Is always so to Woman.

At the Trades Union Congress now being held in London, the Gasworkers' Union moved that instructions be given the Parliamentary Committee to introduce a Bill to prohibit the employment of children under fifteen years of age. Mr. Shackleton, Member of Parliament and a representative of the Northern Counties Weavers, opposed the resolution on behalf of the textile workers, who, he said, could not dispense with the earnings of their children and live on the scale of wages which obtained. The representatives of 514,000 workers voted against the resolution, while the representatives of 535,000 workers voted in favour of it. When 514,000 workers oppose a resolution prohibiting child-labour under fifteen, it is evident that a less-than-living wage is being paid to an immense number of the adult workers of the country.

I have spoken with women in Whitechapel who receive right along less than one shilling for a twelve-hour day in the coat-making sweat shops; and with women trousers finishers who receive an average princely and weekly wage of three to four shillings.

A case recently cropped up of men, in the employ of a wealthy business house, receiving their board and six shillings per week for six working days of sixteen hours each. The sandwich men get fourteenpence per day and find themselves. The average weekly earning of the hawkers and costermongers are not more than ten to twelve shillings. The average of all common labourers, outside the dockers, is less than sixteen shillings per week, while the dockers average from eight to nine shillings. These figures are taken from a royal commission report and are authentic.

Conceive of an old woman, broken and dying, supporting herself and four children, and paying three shillings per week rent, by making match boxes at 2¼d. per gross. Twelve dozen boxes for 2¼d., and, in addition, finding her own paste and thread! She never knew a day off, either for sickness, rest, or recreation. Each day and every day, Sundays as well, she toiled fourteen hours. Her day's stint was seven gross, for which she received 1s. 3¾d. In the week of ninety-eight hours' work, she made 7,066 match boxes, and earned 4s. 10¼d., less per paste and thread.

Last year, Mr. Thomas Holmes, a police-court missionary of note, after writing about the condition of the women workers, received the following letter, dated April 18, 1901:

> Sir, – Pardon the liberty I am taking, but, having read what you said about poor women working fourteen hours a day for ten shillings per week, I beg to state my case. I am a tie-maker, who, after working all the week, cannot earn more than five shillings, and I have a poor afflicted husband to keep who hasn't earned a penny for more than ten years.

Imagine a woman, capable of writing such a clear, sensible, grammatical letter, supporting her husband and self on five shillings per week! Mr. Holmes visited her. He had to squeeze to get into the room. There lay her sick husband; there she worked all day long; there she cooked, ate, washed, and slept; and there her husband and she performed all the functions of living and dying. There was no space for the missionary to sit down, save on the bed, which was partially covered with ties and silk. The sick man's lungs were in the last stages of decay. He coughed and expectorated constantly, the woman ceasing from her work to assist him in his paroxysms. The silken fluff from the ties was not good for his sickness; nor was his sickness good for the ties, and the handlers and wearers of the ties yet to come.

Another case Mr. Holmes visited was that of a young girl, twelve years of age, charged in the police court with stealing food. He found her the deputy mother of a boy of nine, a crippled boy of seven, and a younger child. Her mother was a widow and a blouse-maker. She paid five shillings a week rent. Here are the last items in her house-keeping account: *Tea, ½d.; sugar ½d.; bread, ¼d.; margarine, 1d.; oil, 1½d.; and firewood, ½d.* Good housewives of the soft and tender folk, imagine yourselves marketing and keeping house on such a scale, setting a table for five, and keeping an eye on your deputy mother of twelve to see that she did not steal food for her little brothers and sisters, the while you stitched, stitched, stitched at a nightmare line of blouses, which stretched away into the gloom and down to the pauper's coffin a-yawn for you.

CHAPTER NINETEEN

THE GHETTO

Is it well that while we range with Science, glorying in the time,
City children soak and blacken soul and sense in city slime?
There among the gloomy alleys Progress halts on palsied feet;
Crime and hunger cast out maidens by the thousand on the street;
There the master scrimps his haggard seamstress of her daily bread;
There the single sordid attic holds the living and the dead;
There the smouldering fire of fever creeps across the rotted floor,
And the crowded couch of incest, in the warrens of the poor.

AT one time the nations of Europe confined the undesirable Jews in city ghettos. But today the dominant economic class, by less arbitrary but none the less rigorous methods, has confined the un-desirable yet necessary workers into ghettos of remarkable meanness and vastness. East London is such a ghetto, where the rich and the powerful do not dwell, and the traveller cometh not, and where two million workers swarm, procreate, and die.

It must not be supposed that all the workers of London are crowded into the East End, but the tide is setting strongly in that direction. The poor quarters of the city proper are constantly being destroyed, and the main stream of the unhoused is towards the east. In the last twelve years, one district, 'London over the Border', as it is called, which lies well beyond Aldgate, Whitechapel, and Mile End, has increased 260,000, or over sixty per cent. The churches in this district, by the way, can seat but one in every thirty-seven of the added population.

The City of Dreadful Monotony, the East End is often called, especially by well-fed, optimistic sight-seers, who look over the surface of things and are merely shocked by the intolerable sameness and meanness of it all. If the East End is worthy of no worse title than the City of Dreadful Monotony, and if working people are unworthy of variety and beauty and surprise, it would not be such a bad place in which to live. But the East End does merit a worse title. It should be called The City of Degradation.

While it is not a city of slums, as some people imagine, it may well be said to be one gigantic slum. From the standpoint of simple decency and clean manhood and womanhood, any mean street, of all its mean streets, is a slum. Where sights and sounds abound which neither you nor I would care to have our children see and hear is a place where no man's children should live, and see, and hear. Where you and I would not care to have our wives pass their lives is a place where no other man's wife should have to pass her life. For here, in the East End, the obscenities and brute vulgarities of life are rampant. There is no privacy. The bad corrupts the good, and all fester together. Innocent childhood is sweet and beautiful; but in East London innocence is a fleeting thing, and you must catch them before they crawl out of the cradle, or you will find the very babes as unholily wise as you.

The application of the Golden Rule determines that East London is an unfit place in which to live. Where you would not have your own babe live, and develop, and gather to itself knowledge of life and the things of life, is not a fit place for the babes of other men to live, and develop, and gather to themselves knowledge of life and the things of life. It is a simple thing, this Golden Rule, and all that is required. Political economy and the survival of the fittest can go hang if they say otherwise. What is not good enough for you is not good enough for other men, and there's no more to be said.

There are 300,000 people in London, divided into families, that live in one-room tenements. Far, far more live in two and three rooms and are as badly crowded, regardless of sex, as those that live in one room. The law demands 400 cubic feet of space for each person. In army barracks each soldier is allowed 600 cubic feet. Professor Huxley, at one time himself a medical officer in East London, always held that each person should have 800 cubic feet of space, and that it should be well ventilated with pure air. Yet in London there are 900,000 people living in less than the 400 cubic feet prescribed by the law.

Mr. Charles Booth, who engaged in a systematic work of years in charting and classifying the toiling city population, estimates that there are 1,800,000 people in London who are *poor* and *very poor*. It is of interest to mark what he terms *poor*. By *poor* he means families which have a total weekly income of from eighteen to twenty-one shillings. The *very poor* fall greatly below this standard.

The workers, as a class, are being more and more segregated by their economic masters; and this process, with its jamming and overcrowding, tends not so much towards immorality as unmorality. Here is an extract from a recent meeting of the London County Council, terse and bald, but with a wealth of horror to be read between the lines:

> Mr. Bruce asked the Chairman of the Public Health Committee whether his attention had been called to a number of cases of serious overcrowding in the East End. In St. Georges-in-the-East a man and his wife and their family of eight occupied one small room. This family consisted of five daughters, aged twenty, seventeen, eight, four, and an infant; and three sons, aged fifteen, thirteen, and twelve. In Whitechapel a man and his wife and their three daughters, aged sixteen, eight, and four, and two sons, aged ten and twelve years, occupied a smaller room. In Bethnal Green a man and his wife, with four sons, aged twenty-three, twenty-one, nineteen and sixteen, and two daughters, aged fourteen and seven, were also found in one room. He asked whether it was not the duty of the various local authorities to prevent such serious overcrowding.

But with 900,000 people actually living under illegal conditions, the authorities have their hands full. When the overcrowded folk are ejected they stray off into some other hole; and, as they move their belongings by night, on hand-barrows (one hand-barrow accommodating the entire household goods and the sleeping children), it is next to impossible to keep track of them. If the Public Heath Act of 1891 were suddenly and completely enforced 900,000 people would receive notice to clear out of their houses and go on to the streets, and 500,000 rooms would have to be built before they were all legally housed again.

The mean streets merely look mean from the outside, but inside the walls are to be found squalor, misery, and tragedy. While the following tragedy may be revolting to read, it must not be forgotten that the existence of it is far more revolting.

In Devonshire Place, Lisson Grove, a short while back died an old woman of seventy-five years of age. At the inquest the coroner's officer stated that 'all he found in the room was a lot of old rags covered with vermin. He had got himself smothered with vermin. The room was in a shocking condition, and he had never seen anything like it. Everything was absolutely covered with vermin.'

The doctor said: 'He found deceased lying across the fender on her back. She had one garment and her stockings on. The body was quite alive with vermin, and all the clothes in the room were absolutely grey with insects. Deceased was very badly nourished and was very emaciated. She had extensive sores on her legs, and her stockings were adherent to those sores. The sores were the result of vermin.'

A man present at the inquest wrote: 'I had the evil fortune to see the body of the unfortunate woman as it lay in the mortuary; and even now the memory of that gruesome sight makes me shudder. There she lay in the mortuary shell, so starved and emaciated that she was a mere bundle of skin and bones. Her hair, which was matted with filth, was simply a nest of vermin. Over her bony chest leaped and rolled hundreds, thousands, myriads of vermin.'

If it is not good for your mother and my mother so to die, then it is not good for this woman, whosoever's mother she might be, so to die.

Bishop Wilkinson, who has lived in Zululand, recently said, 'No headman of an African village would allow such a promiscuous mixing of young men and women, boys and girls.' He had reference to the children of the overcrowded folk, who at five have nothing to learn and much to unlearn which they will never unlearn.

It is notorious that here in the Ghetto the houses of the poor are greater profit earners than the mansions of the rich. Not only does the poor worker have to live like a beast, but he pays proportionately more for it than does the rich man for his spacious comfort. A class of house-sweaters has been made possible by the competition of the poor for houses. There are more people than there is room and numbers are in the workhouse because they cannot find shelter elsewhere. Not only are houses let, but they are sublet, and sub-sublet down to the very rooms.

'A part of a room to let.' This notice was posted a short while ago in a window not five minutes' walk from St. James's Hall. The Rev. Hugh Price Hughes, is authority for the statement that beds are let on the three-relay system – that is, three tenants to a bed, each occupying it eight hours, so that it never grows cold; while the floor space underneath the bed is likewise let on the three-relay system. Health officers are not at all unused to finding such cases as the following: in one room having a cubic capacity of 1,000 feet, three adult females in the bed, and two adult females under the bed; and in one room of 1,650 cubic feet, one adult male and two children in the bed, and two adult females under the bed.

Here is a typical example of a room on the more respectable two-relay system. It is occupied in the daytime by a young woman employed all night in a hotel. At seven o'clock in the evening she vacates the room and a bricklayer's labourer comes in. A seven in the morning he vacates, and goes to his work, at which time she returns from hers.

The Rev. W. N. Davies, rector of Spitalfields, took a census of some of the alleys in his parish. He says:

In one alley there are ten houses – fifty-one rooms, nearly all about eight feet by nine feet – and 254 people. In six instances only do two people occupy one room; and in others the number varied from three to nine. In another court with six houses and twenty-two rooms were 84 people – again, six, seven, eight, and nine being the number living in one room, in several instances. In one house with eight rooms are 45 people – one room containing nine persons, one eight, two seven, and another six.

This Ghetto crowding is not through inclination, but compulsion. Nearly fifty per cent of the workers pay from one-fourth to one-half of their earnings for rent. The average rent in the larger part of the East End is from four to six shillings per week for one room, while skilled mechanics, earning thirty-five shillings per week, are forced to part with fifteen shillings of it for two or three pokey little dens, in which they strive desperately to obtain some semblance of home life. And rents are going up all the time. In one street in Stepney the increase in only two years has been from thirteen to eighteen shillings; in another street from eleven to sixteen shillings; and in another street, from eleven to fifteen shillings; while in Whitechapel, two-room houses that recently rented for ten shillings are now costing twenty-one shillings. East, west, north, and south the rents are going up. When land is worth from £20,000 to £30,000 an acre, someone must pay the landlord.

Mr. W. C. Steadman, in the House of Commons, in a speech concerning his constituency in Stepney, related the following:

This morning, not a hundred yards from where I am myself living, a widow stopped me. She has six children to support, and the rent of her house was fourteen shillings per week. She gets her living by letting the house to lodgers and doing a day's washing or charring. That woman, with tears in her eyes, told me that the landlord had increased the rent from fourteen shillings to eighteen shillings. What could the woman do? There is no accommodation in Stepney. Every place is taken up and overcrowded.

Class supremacy can rest only on class degradation; and when the workers are segregated in the Ghetto, they cannot escape the consequent degradation. A short and stunted people is created – a breed strikingly differentiated from their masters' breed, a pavement folk, as it were, lacking stamina and strength. The men become caricatures of what physical men ought to be, and their women and children are pale and anaemic, with eyes ringed darkly, who stoop and slouch, and are early twisted out of all shapeliness and beauty.

To make matters worse, the men of the Ghetto are the men who are left – a deteriorated stock, left to undergo still further deterioration. For a hundred and fifty years, at least, they have been drained of their best. The strong men, the men of pluck, initiative, and ambition, have been faring forth to the fresher and freer portions of the globe, to make new lands and nations. Those who are lacking, the weak of heart and head and hand, as well as the rotten and hopeless, have remained to carry on the breed. And year by year, in turn, the best they breed are taken from them. Wherever a man of vigour and stature manages to grow up, he is haled forthwith into the army. A soldier, as Bernard Shaw has said, 'ostensibly a heroic and patriotic defender of his country, is really an unfortunate man driven by destitution to offer himself as food for powder for the sake of regular rations, shelter, and clothing.'

This constant selection of the best from the workers has impoverished those who are left, a sadly degraded remainder, for the great part, which, in the Ghetto, sinks to the deepest depths. The wine of life has been drawn off to spill itself in blood and progeny over the rest of the earth. Those that remain are the lees, and they are segregated and steeped in themselves. They become indecent and bestial. When they kill, they kill with their hands, and then stupidly surrender themselves to the executioners. There is no splendid audacity about their transgressions. They gouge a mate with a dull knife, or beat his head in with an iron pot, and then sit down and wait for the police. Wife-beating is the masculine prerogative of matrimony. They wear remarkable boots of brass and iron, and when they have polished off the mother of their children with a black eye or so, they knock her down and proceed to trample her very much as a Western stallion tramples a rattlesnake.

A woman of the lower Ghetto classes is as much the slave of her husband as is the Indian squaw. And I, for one, were I a woman and had but the two choices, should prefer being a squaw. The men are economically dependent on their masters, and the women are economically dependent on the men. The result is, the woman gets the beating the man should give his master, and she can do nothing. There are the kiddies, and he is the breadwinner, and she dare not send him to jail and leave herself and children to starve. Evidence to convict can rarely be obtained when such cases come into the courts; as a rule, the trampled wife and mother· is weeping and hysterically beseeching the magistrate to let her husband off for the kiddies' sakes.

The wives become screaming harridans or, broken-spirited and doglike, lose what little decency and self-respect they have remaining over from their maiden days, and all sink together, unheeding, in their degradation and dirt.

Sometimes I become afraid of my own generalizations upon the massed misery of this Ghetto life, and feel that my impressions are exaggerated, that I am too close to the picture and lack perspective. At such moments I find it well to turn to the testimony of other men to prove to myself that I am not becoming overwrought and addle-pated. Frederick Harrison has always struck me as being a level-headed, well-controlled man, and he says:

> To me, at least, it would be enough to condemn modern society as hardly an advance on slavery or serfdom, if the permanent condition of industry were to be that which we behold, that ninety per cent of the actual producers of wealth have no home that they can call their own beyond the end of the week; have no bit of soil, or so much as a room that belongs to them; have nothing of value of any kind, except as much old furniture as will go into a cart; have the precarious chance of weekly wages,

which barely suffice to keep them in health; are housed, for the most part, in places that no man thinks fit for his horse; are separated by so narrow a margin from destitution that a month of bad trade, sickness, or unexpected loss brings them face to face with hunger and pauperism. . . . But below this normal state of the average workman in town and country, there is found the great band of destitute outcasts – the camp followers of the army of industry – at least one-tenth of the whole proletarian population, whose normal condition is one of sickening wretchedness. If this is to be the permanent arrangement of modern society, civilization must be held to bring a curse on the great majority of mankind.

Ninety per cent! The figures are appalling, yet Mr. Stopford Brooke, after drawing a frightful London picture, finds himself compelled to multiply it by half a million. Here it is:

I often used to meet, when I was a curate at Kensington, families drifting into London along the Hammersmith Road. One day there came along a labourer and his wife, his son and two daughters. Their family had lived for a long time on an estate in the country, and managed, with the help of the common-land and their labour, to get on. But the time came when the common was encroached upon, and their labour not needed on the estate, and they were quietly turned out of their cottage. Where should they go? Of course to London, where work was thought to be plentiful. They had a little savings, and they thought they could get two decent rooms to live in. But the inexorable land question met them in London. They tried the decent courts for lodgings, and found that two rooms would cost ten shillings a week. Food was dear and bad, water was bad, and in a short time their health suffered. Work was hard to get, and its wage was so low that they were soon in debt. They became more ill and more despairing with the poisonous surroundings, the darkness, and the long hours of work; and they were driven forth to seek a cheaper lodging. They found it in a court I knew well – a hotbed of crime and nameless horrors. In this they got a single room at a cruel rent, and work was more difficult for them to get now, as they came from a place of such bad repute, and they fell into the hands of those who sweat the last drop out of man and woman and child, for wages which are the food only of despair. And the darkness and the dirt, the bad food and the sickness, and the want of water was worse than before; and the crowd and the companionship of the court robbed them of the last shreds of self-respect. The drink demon seized upon them. Of course there was a public-house at both ends of the court. There they fled, one and all, for shelter, and warmth, and society, and forgetfulness. And they came out in deeper debt, with inflamed senses and burning brains, and an unsatisfied craving for drink they would do anything to satiate. And in a few months the father was in prison, the wife dying, the son a criminal, and the daughters on the street. *Multiply this by half a million, and you will be beneath the truth.*

93

No more dreary spectacle can be found on this earth than the whole of the 'awful East', with its Whitechapel, Hoxton, Spitalfields, Bethnal Green, and Wapping to the East India Docks. The colour of life is grey and drab. Everything is helpless, hopeless, unrelieved, and dirty. Bath tubs are a thing totally unknown, as mythical as the ambrosia of the gods. The people themselves are dirty, while any attempt at cleanliness becomes howling farce, when it is not pitiful and tragic. Strange, vagrant odours come drifting along the greasy wind, and the rain, when it falls, is more like grease than water from heaven. The very cobblestones are scummed with grease.

Here lives a population as dull and unimaginative as its long grey miles of dingy brick. Religion has virtually passed it by, and a gross and stupid materialism reigns, fatal alike to the things of the spirit and the finer instincts of life.

It used to be the proud boast that every Englishman's home was his castle. But today it is an anachronism. The Ghetto folk have no homes. They do not know the significance and the sacredness of home life. Even the municipal dwellings, where live the better-class workers, are over-crowded barracks. They have no home life. The very language proves it. The father returning from work asks his child in the street where her mother is; and back the answer comes, 'In the buildings.'

A new race has sprung up, a street people. They pass their lives at work and in the streets. They have dens and lairs into which to crawl for sleeping purposes, and that is all. One cannot travesty the word by calling such dens and lairs 'homes'. The traditional silent and reserved Englishman has passed away. The pavement folk are noisy, voluble, high-strung, excitable – when they are yet young. As they grow older they become steeped and stupefied in beer. When they have nothing else to do, they ruminate as a cow ruminates. They are to be met with everywhere, standing on curbs and corners, and staring into vacancy. Watch one of them. He will stand there, motionless, for hours, and when you go away you will leave him still staring into vacancy. It is most absorbing. He has no money for beer, and his lair is only for sleeping purposes, so what else remains for him to do? He has already solved the mysteries of girl's love, and wife's love, and child's love, and found them delusions and shams, vain and fleeting as dewdrops, quick-vanishing before the ferocious facts of life.

As I say, the young are high-strung, nervous, excitable; the middle aged are empty-headed, stolid, and stupid. It is absurd to think for an instant that they can compete with the workers of the New World. Brutalized, degraded, and dull, the Ghetto folk will be unable to render efficient service to England in the world struggle for industrial supremacy which economists declare has already begun. Neither as workers nor as soldiers can they come up to the mark when England, in her need, calls upon them, her forgotten ones; and if England be flung out of the world's industrial orbit, they will perish like flies at the end of summer. Or, with England critically situated, and with them made desperate as wild beasts are made desperate, they may become a menace and go 'swelling' down to the West End to return the 'slumming' the West End has done in the East. In which case, before rapid-fire guns and the modern machinery of warfare, they will perish the more swiftly and easily.

CHAPTER TWENTY

COFFEE-HOUSES AND DOSS-HOUSES

ANOTHER phrase gone glimmering, shorn of romance and tradition and all that goes to make phrases worth keeping! For me, henceforth, 'coffee-house' will possess anything but an agreeable connotation. Over on the other side of the world, the mere mention of the word was sufficient to conjure up whole crowds of its historic frequenters, and to send trooping through my imagination endless groups of wits and dandies, pamphleteers and bravos, and Bohemians of Grub Street.

But here, on this side of the world, alas and alack, the very name is a misnomer. Coffee-house: a place where people drink coffee. Not at all. You cannot obtain coffee in such a place for love or money. True, you may call for coffee, and you will have brought you something in a cup purporting to be coffee, and you will taste it and be disillusioned, for coffee it certainly is not.

And what is true of the coffee is true of the coffee-house. Working-men, in the main, frequent these places, and greasy, dirty places they are, without one thing about them to cherish decency in a man or put self-respect into him. Table-cloths and napkins are unknown. A man eats in the midst of the débris left by his predecessor, and dribbles his own scraps about him and on the floor. In rush times, in such places, I have positively waded through the muck and mess that covered the floor, and I have managed to eat because I was abominably hungry and capable of eating anything.

This seems to be the normal condition of the working-man, from the zest with which he addresses himself to the board. Eating is a necessity, and there are no frills about it. He brings in with him a primitive voraciousness, and, I am confident, carries away with him a fairly healthy appetite. When you see such a man, on his way to work in the morning, order a pint of tea, which is no more tea than it is ambrosia, pull a hunk of dry bread from his pocket, and wash the one down with the other, depend upon it, that man has not the right sort of stuff in his belly, nor enough of the wrong sort of stuff, to fit him for his day's work. And further, depend upon it, he and a thousand of his kind will not turn out the quantity or quality of work that a thousand men will who have eaten heartily of meat and potatoes, and drunk coffee that is coffee.

As a vagrant in the 'Hobo' of a California jail, I have been served better food and drink than the London workman receives in his coffee-houses; while as an American labourer I have eaten a breakfast for twelvepence such as the British labourer would not dream of eating. Of course, he will pay only three or four pence for his; which is, however, as much as I paid, for I would be earning six shillings to his two or two and a half. On the other hand, though, and in return, I would turn out an amount of work in the course of the day that would put to shame the amount he turned out. So there are two sides to it. The man with the high standard of living will always do more work and better than the man with the low standard of living.

There is a comparison which sailormen make between the English and American merchant services. In an English ship, they say, it is poor grub, poor pay, and easy work; in an American ship, good grub, good pay, and hard work. And this is applicable to the working populations of both countries. The ocean greyhounds have to pay for speed and steam, and so does the workman. But if the workman is not able to pay for it, he will not have the speed and steam, that is all. The proof of it is when the English workman comes to America. He will lay more bricks in New York than he will in London, still more bricks in St. Louis, and still more bricks when he gets to San Francisco.* His standard of living has been rising all the time.

Early in the morning, along the streets frequented by workmen on the way to work, many women sit on the sidewalk with sacks of bread beside them. No end of workmen purchase these, and eat them as they walk along. They do not even wash the dry bread down with the tea to be obtained for a penny in the coffee-houses. It is incontestable that a man is not fit to begin his day's work on a meal like that; and it is equally incontestable that the loss will fall upon his employer and upon the nation. For some time now, statesmen have been crying, 'Wake up, England!' It would show more hard-headed common sense if they changed the tune to 'Feed up, England!'

Not only is the worker poorly fed, but he is filthily fed. I have stood outside a butcher-shop and watched a horde of speculative housewives turning over the trimmings and scraps and shreds of beef and mutton – dog-meat in the States. I would not vouch for the clean fingers of these housewives, no more than I would vouch for the cleanliness of the single rooms in which many of them and their families lived; yet they raked, and pawed, and scraped the mess about in their anxiety to get the worth of their coppers. I kept my eye on one particularly offensive-looking bit of meat, and followed it through the clutches of over twenty women, till it fell to the lot of a timid-appearing little woman whom the butcher bluffed into taking it. All day long this heap of scraps was added to and taken away from, the dust and dirt of the street falling upon it, flies settling on it, and the dirty fingers turning it over and over.

The costers wheel loads of specked and decaying fruit around in the barrows all day, and very often store it in their one living and sleeping room for the night. There it is exposed to the sickness and disease, the effluvia and vile exhalations of overcrowded and rotten life, and next day it is carted about again to be sold.

* The San Francisco bricklayer receives twenty shillings per day, and at present is on strike for twenty-four shillings.

The poor worker of the East End never knows what it is to eat good, wholesome meat or fruit – in fact, he rarely eats meat or fruit at all; while the skilled workman has nothing to boast of in the way of what he eats. Judging from the coffee-houses, which is a fair criterion, they never know in all their lives what tea, coffee, or cocoa tastes like. The slops and water-witcheries of the coffee-houses, varying only in sloppiness and witchery, never even approximate or suggest what you and I are accustomed to drink as tea and coffee.

A little incident comes to me, connected with a coffee-house not far from Jubilee Street on the Mile End Road.

'Cawn yer let me 'ave somthin' for this, daughter? Anythin', Hi don't mind. Hi 'aven't 'ad a bite the blessed dy, an' Hi'm that fynt . . .'

She was an old woman, clad in decent black rags, and in her hand she held a penny. The one she had addressed as 'daughter' was a careworn woman of forty, proprietress and waitress of the house.

I waited, possibly as anxiously as the old woman, to see how the appeal would be received. It was four in the afternoon, and she looked faint and sick. The woman hesitated an instant, then brought a large plate of 'stewed lamb and young peas'. I was eating a plate of it myself, and it is my judgment that the lamb was mutton and that the peas might have been younger without being youthful. However, the point is, the dish was sold at sixpence, and the proprietress gave it for a penny, demonstrating anew the old truth that the poor are the most charitable.

The old woman, profuse in her gratitude, took a seat on the other side of the narrow table and ravenously attacked the smoking stew. We ate steadily and silently, the pair of us, when suddenly, explosively and most gleefully, she cried out to me,—

'Hi sold a box o' matches! Yes,' she confirmed, if anything with greater and more explosive glee. 'Hi sold a box o' matches! That's 'ow Hi got the penny.'

'You must be getting along in years,' I suggested.

'Seventy-four yesterday,' she replied, and returned with gusto to her plate.

'Blimey, I'd like to do something for the old girl, that I would, but this is the first I've 'ad tody,' the young fellow alongside volunteered to me. 'An' I only 'ave this because I 'appened to make an odd shilling washin' out. Lord lumme! I don't know 'ow many pots.

'No work at my own tryde for six weeks,' he said further, in reply to my question; 'nothin but odd jobs a blessed long wy between.'

One meets with all sorts of adventures in coffee-houses, and I shall not soon forget a Cockney Amazon in a place near Trafalgar Square, to whom I tendered a sovereign when paying my score. (By the way, one is supposed to pay before he begins to eat, and if he be poorly dressed he is compelled to pay before he eats.)

The girl bit the gold piece between her teeth, rang it on the counter and then looked me and my rags witheringly up and down.

'Where'd you find it?' she at length demanded.

'Some mug left it on the table when he went out, eh, don't you think?' I retorted.

'Wot's yer gyme?' she queried, looking me calmly in the eyes.

'I makes 'em,' quoth I.

She sniffed superciliously and gave me the change in small silver, and I had my revenge by biting and ringing every piece of it.

'I'll give you a ha'penny for another lump of sugar in the tea,' I said.

'I'll see you in 'ell first,' came the retort courteous. Also, she amplified the retort courteous in divers vivid and unprintable ways.

I never had much talent for repartee, but she knocked silly what little I had, and I gulped down my tea a beaten man, while she gloated after me even as I passed out to the street.

While 300,000 people of London live in one-room tenements, and 900,000 are illegally and viciously housed, 38,000 more are registered as living in common lodging-houses – known in the vernacular as 'doss-houses'. There are many kinds of doss-houses, but in one thing they are all alike, from the filthy little ones to the monster big ones paying five per cent and blatantly lauded by smug middle-class men who know but one thing about them, and that one thing is their uninhabitableness. By this I do not mean that the roofs leak or the walls are draughty; but what I do mean is that life in them is degrading and unwholesome.

'The poor man's hotel,' they are often called, but the phrase is caricature. Not to possess a room to one's self, in which sometimes to sit alone; to be forced out of bed willy-nilly, the first thing in the morning; to engage and pay anew for a bed each night; and never to have any privacy, surely is a mode of existence quite different from that of hotel life.

This must not be considered a sweeping condemnation of the big private and municipal lodging-houses and working-men's homes. Far from it. They have remedied many of the atrocities attendant upon the irresponsible small doss-houses, and they give the workman more for his money than he ever received before; but that does not make them as habitable or wholesome as the dwelling-place of a man should be who does his work in the world.

The little private doss-houses, as a rule, are unmitigated horrors. I have slept in them, and I know; but let me pass them by and confine myself to the bigger and better ones. Not far from Middlesex Street, Whitechapel, I entered such a house, a place inhabited almost entirely by working men. The entrance was by way of a flight of steps descending from the side-walk to what was properly the cellar of the building. Here were two large and gloomily lighted rooms, in which men cooked and ate. I had intended to do some cooking myself, but the smell of the place stole away my appetite, or, rather, wrested it from me; so I contented myself with watching other men cook and eat.

One workman, home from work, sat down opposite me at the rough wooden table, and began his meal. A handful of salt on the not over-clean table constituted his butter. Into it he dipped his bread, mouthful by mouthful, and washed it down with tea from a big mug. A piece of fish completed his bill of fare. He ate silently, looking neither to right nor left nor across at me. Here and there, at the various tables, other men were eating, just as silently. In the whole room there was hardly a note of conversation. A feeling of gloom pervaded the ill-lighted place. Many of them sat and brooded over the crumbs of their repast, and made me wonder, as Childe Roland wondered, what evil they had done that they should be punished so.

From the kitchen came the sounds of more genial life, and I ventured into the range where the men were cooking. But the smell I had noticed on entering was stronger here, and a rising nausea drove me into the street for fresh air.

On my return I paid fivepence for a 'cabin', took my receipt for the same in the form of a huge brass check, and went upstairs to the smoking-room. Here, a couple of small billiard tables and several checkerboards were being used by young working-men, who waited in relays for their turn at the games, while many men were sitting around, smoking, reading, and mending their clothes. The young men were hilarious, the old men were gloomy. In fact, there were two types of men, the cheerful and the sodden or blue, and age seemed to determine the classification.

But no more than the two cellar rooms did this room convey the remotest suggestion of home. Certainly there could be nothing homelike about it to you and me, who know what home really is. On the walls were the most preposterous and insulting notices regulating the conduct of the guests, and at ten o'clock the lights were put out, and nothing remained but bed. This was gained by descending again to the cellar, by surrendering the brass check to a burly doorkeeper, and by climbing a long flight of stairs into the upper regions. I went to the top of the building and down again, passing several floors filled with sleeping men. The 'cabins' were the best accommodation, each cabin allowing space for a tiny bed and room alongside of it in which to undress. The bedding was clean, and with neither it nor the bed do I find any fault. But there was no privacy about it, no being alone.

To get an adequate idea of a floor filled with cabins, you have merely to magnify a layer of the pasteboard pigeon-holes of an eggcrate till each pigeon-hole is seven feet in height and otherwise properly dimensioned, then place the magnified layer on the floor of a large, barnlike room, and there you have it. There are no ceilings to the pigeon-holes, the walls are thin, and the snores from all the sleepers and every move and turn of your nearer neighbours come plainly to your ears. And this cabin is yours only for a little while. In the morning out you go. You cannot put your trunk in it, or come and go when you like, or lock the door behind you, or anything of the sort. In fact there is no door at all, only a doorway. If you care to remain a guest in this poor man's hotel, you must put up with all this, and with prison regulations which impress upon you constantly that you are nobody, with little soul of your own and less to say about it.

Now I contend that the least a man who does his day's work should have is a room to himself, where he can lock the door and be safe in his possessions; where he can sit down and read by a window or look out; where he can come and go whenever he wishes; where he can accumulate a few personal belongings other than those he carries about with him on his back and in his pockets; where he can hang up pictures of his mother, sister, sweetheart, ballet dancers, or bulldogs, as his heart listeth – in short, one place of his own on the earth of which he can say: 'This is mine, my castle; the world stops at the threshold; here am I lord and master.' He will be a better citizen, this man; and he will do a better day's work.

I stood on one floor of the poor man's hotel and listened. I went from bed to bed and looked at the sleepers. They were young men, from twenty to forty, most of them. Old men cannot afford the working-man's home. They go to the workhouse. But I looked at the young men, scores of them, and they were not bad-looking fellows. Their faces were made for women's kisses, their necks for women's arms. They were lovable, as men are lovable. They were capable of love. A woman's touch redeems and softens, and they needed such redemption and softening instead of each day growing harsh and harsher. And I wondered where these women were, and heard a 'harlot's ginny laugh'. Leman Street, Waterloo Road, Piccadilly, The Strand, answered me, and I knew where they were.

CHAPTER TWENTY-ONE

THE PRECARIOUSNESS OF LIFE

I WAS talking with a very vindictive man. In his opinion, his wife had wronged him and the law had wronged him. The merits and morals of the case are immaterial. The meat of the matter is that she had obtained a separation, and he was compelled to pay ten shillings each week for the support of her and the five children. 'But look you,' said he to me, 'wot'll 'appen to 'er if I don't py up the ten shillings? S'posin', now, just s'posin' a accident 'appens to me, so I cawnt work. Sposin' I get a rupture, or the rheumatics, or the cholera. Wot's she goin' to do, eh. Wot's she goin' to do?'

He shook his head sadly. 'No 'ope for 'er. The best she cawn do is the work'ouse, an' that's 'ell. An if she don't go to the work'ouse, it'll be a worse 'ell. Come along wi me an' I'll show you women sleepin' in a passage, a dozen of 'em. An' I'll show you worse, wot she'll come to if anythin' 'appens to me and the ten shillings.'

The certitude of this man's forecast is worthy of consideration. He knew conditions sufficiently to know the precariousness of his wife's grasp on food and shelter. For her game was up when his working capacity was impaired or destroyed. And when this state of affair is looked at in its larger aspect, the same will be found true of hundreds of thousands and even millions of men and women living amicably together and co-operating in the pursuit of food and shelter.

The figures are appalling: 1,800,000 people in London live on the poverty line and below it, and 1,000,000 live with one week's wages between them and pauperism. In all England and Wales, eighteen per cent of the whole population are driven to the parish for relief, and in London, according to the statistics of the London County Council, twenty-one per cent of the whole population are driven to the parish for relief. Between being driven to the parish for relief and being an out-and-out pauper there is a great difference, yet London supports 123,000 paupers, quite a city of folk in themselves. One in every four in London dies on public charity, while 939 out of every 1,000 in the United Kingdom die in poverty; 8,000,000 simply struggle on the ragged edge of starvation, and 20,000,000 more are not comfortable in the simple and clean sense' of the word.

It is interesting to go more into detail concerning the London people who die on charity.

In 1886, and up to 1893, the percentage of pauperism to population was less in London than in all England; but since 1893, and for every succeeding year, the percentage of pauperism to population has been greater in London than in all England. Yet, from the Registrar-General's Report for 1886, the following figures are taken:

Out of 81,951 deaths in London (1884):

In workhouses	9,909
In hospitals	6,559
In lunatic asylums	278
Total in public refuges	16,746

Commenting on these figures, a Fabian writer says: 'Considering that comparatively few of these are children, it is probable that one in every three London adults will be driven into one of these refuges to die, and the proportion in the case of the manual labour class must of course be still larger.'

These figures serve somewhat to indicate the proximity of the average worker to pauperism. Various things make pauperism. An advertisement, for instance, such as this, appearing in yesterday's morning's paper:

'Clerk wanted, with knowledge of shorthand, type-writing, and invoicing: wages ten shillings ($2.50) a week. Apply by letter,' &c.

And in today's paper I read of a clerk, thirty-five years of age and an inmate of a London workhouse, brought before a magistrate for non-performance of task. He claimed that he had done his various tasks since he had been an inmate; but when the master set him to breaking stones, his hands blistered, and he could not finish the task. He had never been used to an implement heavier than a pen, he said. The magistrate sentenced him and his blistered hands to seven days' hard labour.

Old age, of course, makes pauperism. And then there is the

accident, the thing happening, the death or disablement of the husband, father, and bread-winner. Here is a man, with a wife and three children, living on the ticklish security of twenty shillings per week – and there are hundreds of thousands of such families in London. Perforce, to even half exist, they must live up to the last penny of it, so that a week's wages (one pound) is all that stands between this family and pauperism or starvation. The thing happens, the father is struck down, and what then? A mother with three children can do little or nothing. Either she must hand her children over to society as juvenile paupers, in order to be free to do something adequate for herself, or she must go to the sweat-shops for work which she can perform in the vile den possible to her reduced income. But with the sweat-shops, married women who eke out their husbands' earnings, and single women who have but themselves miserably to support, determine the scale of wages. And this scale of wages, so determined, is so low that the mother and her three children can live only in positive beastliness and semi-starvation, till decay and death end their suffering.

To show that this mother, with her three children to support, cannot compete in the sweating industries, I instance from the current newspapers the two following cases:

A father indignantly writes that his daughter and a girl companion receive 8½d. per gross for making boxes. They made each day four gross. Their expenses were 8d. for car fare, 2d. for stamps, 2½d. for glue, and 1d. for string, so that all they earned between them was 1s. 9d., or a daily wage each of 10½d.

In the second case, before the Luton Guardians a few days ago, an old woman of seventy-two appeared, asking for relief. 'She was a straw-hat maker, but had been compelled to give up the work owing to the price she obtained for them – namely 2¼d. each. For that price she had to provide plait trimmings and make and finish the hats'.

Yet this mother and her three children we are considering have done no wrong that they should be so punished. They have not sinned. The thing happened, that is all; the husband, father and bread-winner, was struck down. There is no guarding against it. It is fortuitous. A family stands so many chances of escaping the bottom of the Abyss, and so many chances of falling plump down to it. The chance is reducible to cold, pitiless figures, and a few of these figures will not be out of place.

Sir A. Forwood calculates that—

1 of every 1,400 workmen is killed annually.
1 of every 2,500 workmen is totally disabled.
1 of every 300 workmen is permanently partially disabled.
1 of every 8 workmen is temporarily disabled three or four weeks.

But these are only the accidents of industry. The high mortality of the people who live in the Ghetto plays a terrible part. The average age at death among the people of the West End is fifty-five years; the average age at death among the people of the East End is thirty years. That is to say, the person in the West End has twice the chance for life that the person has in the East End. Talk of war! The mortality in South Africa and the Philippines fades away to insignificance. Here, in the heart of peace, is where the blood is being shed; and here not even the civilized rules of warfare obtain, for the women and children and babes in the arms are killed just as ferociously as the men are killed. War! In England, every year, 500,000 men, women, and children, engaged in the various industries, are killed and disabled, or are injured to disablement by disease.

In the West End eighteen per cent of the children die before five years of age; in the East End fifty-five per cent of the children die before five years of age. And there are streets in London where, out of every one hundred children born in a year, fifty die during the next year; and of the fifty that remain, twenty-five die before they are five years old. Slaughter! Herod did not do quite so badly.

That industry causes greater havoc with human life than battles does no better substantiation can be given than the following extract from a recent report of the Liverpool Medical Officer, which is not applicable to Liverpool alone:

> In many instances little if any sunlight could get to the courts, and the atmosphere within the dwellings was always foul, owing largely to the saturated condition of the walls and ceilings, which for so many years had absorbed the exhalations of the occupants into their porous material. Singular testimony to the absence of sunlight in these courts was furnished by the action of the Parks and Gardens Committee, who desires to brighten the homes of the poorest class by gifts of growing flowers and window-boxes; but these gifts could not be made in courts such as these, *as flowers and plants were susceptible to the unwholesome surroundings, and would not live.*

Mr. George Haw has compiled the following table on the three St. George's parishes (London parishes):

	Percentage of Overcrowded Population	Death-rate per 1,000
St. George's West . .	10	13.2
St. George's South . .	35	23.7
St. George's East . .	40	26.4

Then there are the 'dangerous trades', in which countless workers are employed. Their hold on life is indeed precarious – far, far more precarious than the hold of the twentieth-century soldier on life. In the linen trade, in the preparation of the flax, wet feet and wet clothes cause an unusual amount of bronchitis, pneumonia, and severe rheumatism; while in the carding and spinning departments the fine dust produces lung disease in the majority of cases, and the woman who starts carding at seventeen or eighteen begins to break up and go to pieces at thirty. The chemical labourers, picked from the strongest and most splendidly-built men to be found, live, on an average, less than forty-eight years.

Says Dr. Arlidge, of the potter's trade: 'Potter's dust does not kill suddenly, but settles, year after year, a little more firmly into the lungs, until at length a case of plaster is formed. Breathing becomes more and more difficult and depressed, and finally ceases.'

Steel dust, stone dust, clay dust, alkali dust, fluff dust, fibre dust – all these things kill, and they are more deadly than machine-guns and pom-poms. Worst of all is the lead dust in the white-lead trades. Here is a description of the typical dissolution of a young, healthy, well-developed girl who goes to work in a white-lead factory:

Here, after a varying degree of exposure, she becomes anaemic. It may be that her gums show a very faint blue line, or perchance her teeth and gums are perfectly sound, and no blue line is discernible. Coincidently with the anaemia she has been getting thinner, but so gradually as scarcely to impress itself upon her or her friends. Sickness, however, ensues, and headaches, growing in intensity, are developed. These are frequently attended by obscuration of vision or temporary blindness. Such a girl passes into what appears to her friends and medical adviser as ordinary hysteria. This gradually deepens without warning, until she is suddenly seized with a convulsion, beginning in one half of the face, then involving the arm, next the leg of the same side of the body, until the convulsion, violent and purely epileptic form in character, becomes universal. This is attended by loss of consciousness, out of which she passes into a series of convulsions, gradually increasing in severity, in one of which she dies – or consciousness, partial or perfect, is regained, either, it may be, for a few minutes, a few hours, or days, during which violent headache is complained of, or she is delirious and excited, as in acute mania, or dull and sullen as in melancholia, and requires to be roused, when she is found wandering, and her speech is somewhat imperfect. Without further warning, save that the pulse, which has become soft, with nearly the normal number of beats, all at once becomes low and hard; she is suddenly seized with another convulsion, in which she dies, or passes into a state of coma from which she never rallies. In another case the convulsions will gradually subside, the headache disappears and the patient recovers, only to find that she had completely lost her eyesight, a loss that may be temporary or permanent.

And here are a few specific cases of white-lead poisoning:
Charlotte Rafferty, a fine, well-grown young woman with a splendid constitution – who had never had a day's illness in her life – became a white-lead worker. Convulsions seized her at the foot of the ladder in the works. Dr. Oliver examined her, found the blue lines along her gums, which shows that the system is under the influence of the

lead. He knew that the convulsions would shortly return. They did so, and she died.

Mary Ann Toler – a girl of seventeen, who had never had a fit in her life – three times became ill, and had to leave off work in the factory. Before she was nineteen she showed symptoms of lead poisoning – had fits, frothed at the mouth, and died.

Mary A., an unusually vigorous woman, was able to work in the lead factory for *twenty years*, having colic once only during that time. Her eight children all died in early infancy from convulsions. One morning, whilst brushing her hair, this woman suddenly lost all power in both her wrists.

Eliza H., aged twenty-five, *after five months* at lead works, was seized with colic. She entered another factory (after being refused by the first one) and worked on uninterruptedly for two years. Then the former symptoms returned, she was seized with convulsions, and died in two days of acute lead poisoning.

Mr. Vaughan Nash, speaking of the unborn generation, says: 'The children of the white-lead worker enter the world, as a rule, only to die from the convulsions of lead poisoning – they are either born prematurely, or die within the first year.'

And, finally, let me instance the case of Harriet A. Walker, a young girl of seventeen, killed while leading a forlorn hope on the industrial battlefield. She was employed as an enamelled ware brusher, where lead poisoning is encountered. Her father and brother were both out of employment. She concealed her illness, walked six miles a day to and from work, earned her seven or eight shillings per week, and died, at seventeen.

Depression in trade also plays an important part in hurling the workers into the Abyss. With a week's wages between a family and pauperism, a month's enforced idleness means hardship and misery almost indescribable, and from the ravages of which the victims do not always recover when work is to be had again. Just now the daily papers contain the report of a meeting of the Carlisle branch of the Dockers' Union, wherein it is stated that many of the men, for months past, have not averaged a weekly income of more than from four to five shillings. The stagnated state of the shipping industry in the port of London is held accountable for this condition of affairs.

To the young working-man or working-woman, or married couple, there is no assurance of happy or healthy middle life, nor of solvent old age. Work as they will, they cannot make their future secure. It is all a matter of chance. Everything depends upon the thing happening, the thing with which they have nothing to do. Precaution cannot fend it off, nor can wiles evade it. If they remain on the industrial battlefield they must face it and take their chance against heavy odds. Of course, if they are favourably made and are not tied by kinship duties, they may run away from the industrial battlefield. In which event the safest thing the man can do is to join the army; and for the woman, possibly, to become a Red Cross nurse or go into a nunnery. In either case they must forego home and children and all that makes life worth living and old age other than a nightmare.

CHAPTER TWENTY-TWO

SUICIDE

WITH life so precarious, and opportunity for the happiness of life so remote, it is inevitable that life shall be cheap and suicide common. So common is it, that one cannot pick up a daily paper without running across it; while an attempt-at-suicide case in a police court excites no more interest than an ordinary 'drunk', and is handled with the same rapidity and unconcern.

I remember such a case in the Thames Police Court. I pride myself that I have good eyes and ears, and a fair working knowledge of men and things; but I confess, as I stood in that court-room, that I was half bewildered by the amazing despatch with which drunks, disorderlies, vagrants, brawlers, wife-beaters, thieves, fences, gamblers, and women of the street went through the machine of justice. The dock stood in the centre of the court (where the light is best), and into it and out again stepped men, women, and children, in a stream as steady as the stream of sentences which fell from the magistrate's lips.

I was still pondering over a consumptive 'fence' who had pleaded inability to work and necessity for supporting wife and children, and who had received a year at hard labour, when a young boy of about twenty appeared in the dock. 'Alfred Freeman,' I caught his name, but failed to catch the charge. A stout and motherly-looking woman bobbed up in the witness-box and began her testimony. Wife of the Britannia lock-keeper, I learned she was. Time, night; a splash; she ran to the lock and found the prisoner in the water.

I flashed my gaze from her to him. So that was the charge, self-murder. He stood there dazed and unheeding, his bonny brown hair rumpled down his forehead, his face haggard and careworn and boyish still.

'Yes, sir,' the lock-keeper's wife was saying. 'As fast as I pulled to get 'im out, 'e crawled back. Then I called for 'elp, and some workmen 'appened along, and we got 'im out and turned 'im over to the constable.'

The magistrate complimented the woman on her muscular powers, and the court-room laughed; but all I could see was a boy on the threshold of life, passionately crawling to muddy death, and there was no laughter in it.

A man was now in the witness-box, testifying to the boy's good character and giving extenuating evidence. He was the boy's foreman, or had been. Alfred was a good boy, but he had had lots of trouble at home, money matters. And then his mother was sick. He was given to worrying and he worried over it till he laid himself out and wasn't fit for work. He (the foreman), for the sake of his own reputation, the boy's work being bad, had been forced to ask him to resign.

'Anything to say?' the magistrate demanded abruptly.

The boy in the dock mumbled something indistinctly. He was still dazed.

'What does he say, constable?' the magistrate asked impatiently.

The stalwart man in blue bent his ear to the prisoner's lips, and then replied loudly, 'He says he's very sorry, your Worship.'

'Remanded,' said his Worship; and the next case was under way, the first witness already engaged in taking the oath. The boy, dazed and unheeding, passed out with the gaoler. That was all, five minutes from start to finish; and two hulking brutes in the dock were trying strenuously to shift the responsibility of the possession of a stolen fishing-pole, worth probably ten cents.

The chief trouble with these poor folk is that they do not know how to commit suicide, and usually have to make two or three attempts before they succeed. This, very naturally, is a horrid nuisance to the constables and magistrates, and gives them no end of trouble. Sometimes, however, the magistrates are frankly outspoken about the matter, and censure the prisoners for the slackness of their attempts. For instance, Mr. R. S—, chairman of the S— B— magistrates, in the case the other day of Ann Wood, who tried to make away with herself in the canal: 'If you wanted to do it, why didn't you do it and get it done with?' demanded the indignant Mr. R. S—. 'Why did you not get under the water and make an end of it, instead of giving us all this trouble and bother?'

Poverty, misery, and fear of the workhouse, are the principal causes of suicide among the working classes. 'I'll drown myself before I go into the workhouse,' said Ellen Hughes Hunt, aged fifty-two. Last Wednesday they held an inquest on her body at Shoreditch. Her husband came from the Islington Workhouse to testify. He had been a cheesemonger, but failure in business and poverty had driven him into the workhouse, whither his wife had refused to accompany him.

She was last seen at one in the morning. Three hours later her hat and jacket were found on the towing path by the Regent's Canal, and later her body was fished from the water. *Verdict: Suicide during temporary insanity*.

Such verdicts are crimes against truth. The Law is a lie, and through it men lie most shamelessly. For instance, a disgraced woman, forsaken and spat upon by kith and kin, doses herself and her baby with laudanum. The baby dies; but she pulls through after a few weeks in hospital, is charged with murder, convicted, and sentenced to ten years' penal servitude. Recovering, the Law holds her responsible for her actions; yet, had she died, the same Law would have rendered a verdict of temporary insanity.

Now, considering the case of Ellen Hughes Hunt, it is as fair and logical to say that her husband was suffering from temporary insanity when he went into the Islington Workhouse, as it is to say that she was suffering from temporary insanity when she went into the Regent's Canal. As to which is the preferable sojourning place is a matter of opinion, of intellectual judgment. I, for one, from what I know of canals and workhouses, should choose the canal, were I in a similar position. And I make bold to contend that I am no more insane than Ellen Hughes Hunt, her husband, and the rest of the human herd.

Man no longer follows instinct with the old natural fidelity. He has developed into a reasoning creature, and can intellectually cling to life or discard life just as life happens to promise great pleasure or pain. I dare to assert that Ellen Hughes Hunt, defrauded and bilked of all the joys of life which fifty-two years' service in the world has earned, with nothing but the horrors of the workhouse before her, was very rational and level-headed when she elected to jump into the canal. And I dare to assert, further, that the jury had done a wiser thing to bring in a verdict charging society with temporary insanity for allowing Ellen Hughes Hunt to be defrauded and bilked of all the joys of life which fifty-two years' service in the world had earned.

Temporary insanity! Oh, these cursed phrases, these lies of language, under which people with meat in their bellies and whole shirts on their backs shelter themselves, and evade the responsibility of their brothers and sisters, empty of belly and without whole shirts on their backs.

From one issue of the *Observer*, an East End paper, I quote the following commonplace events:

A ship's fireman, named Johnny King, was charged with attempting to commit suicide. On Wednesday defendant went to Bow Police Station and stated that he had swallowed a quantity of phosphor paste, as he was hard up and unable to obtain work. King was taken inside and an emetic administered, when he vomited up a quantity of the poison. Defendant now said he was very sorry. Although he had sixteen years' good character, he was unable to obtain work of any kind. Mr. Dickinson had defendant put back for the court missionary to see him.

Timothy Warner, thirty-two, was remanded for a similar offence. He jumped off Limehouse Pier, and when rescued, said, 'I intended to do it.'

A decent-looking young woman, named Ellen Gray, was remanded on a charge of attempting to commit suicide. About half-past eight on Sunday morning Constable 834 K found defendant lying in a doorway in Benworth Street, and she was in a very drowsy condition. She was holding an empty bottle in one hand, and stated that some two or three hours previously she had swallowed a quantity of laudanum. As she was evidently very ill, the divisional surgeon was sent for, and having administered some coffee, ordered that she was to be kept awake. When defendant was charged, she stated that the reason why she attempted to take her life was she had neither home nor friends.

I do not say that all people who commit suicide are sane, no more than I say that all people who do not commit suicide are sane. Insecurity of food and shelter, by the way, is a great cause of insanity among the living. Costermongers, hawkers, and pedlars, a class of workers who live from hand to mouth more than those of any other class, form the highest percentage of those in the lunatic asylums. Among the males each year, 26.9 per 10,000 go insane, and among the women, 36.9. On the other hand, of soldiers, who are at least sure of food and shelter, 13 per 10,000 go insane; and of farmers and graziers, only 5.1. So a coster is twice as likely to lose his reason as a soldier, and five times as likely as a farmer.

Misfortune and misery are very potent in turning people's heads, and drive one person to the lunatic asylum, and another to the morgue or the gallows. When the thing happens, and the father and husband, for all of his love for wife and children and his willingness to work, can get no work to do, it is a simple matter for his reason to totter and the light within his brain go out. And it is especially simple when it is taken into consideration that his body is ravaged by innutrition and disease, in addition to his soul being torn by the sight of his suffering wife and little ones.

'He is a good-looking man, with a mass of black hair, dark, expressive eyes, delicately chiselled nose and chin, and wavy, fair moustache.' This is the reporter's description of Frank Cavilla as he stood in court, this dreary month of September, 'dressed in a much worn grey suit, and wearing no collar.'

Frank Cavilla lived and worked as a house decorator in London. He is described as a good workman, a steady fellow, and not given to drink, while all his neighbours unite in testifying that he was a gentle and affectionate husband and father.

His wife, Hannah Cavilla, was a big, handsome, light-hearted woman. She saw to it that his children were sent neat and clean (the neighbours all remarked on the fact) to the Childeric Road Board School. And so, with such a man, so blessed, working steadily and living temperately, all went well, and the goose hung high.

Then the thing happened. He worked for a Mr. Beck, builder, and lived in one of his master's houses in Trundley Road. Mr. Beck was thrown from his trap and killed. The thing was an unruly horse, and, as I say, it happened. Cavilla had to seek fresh employment and find another house.

This occurred eighteen months ago. For eighteen months he fought the big fight. He got rooms in a little house in Batavia Road, but could not make both ends meet. Steady work could not be obtained. He struggled manfully at casual employment of all sorts, his wife and four children starving before his eyes. He starved himself, and grew weak, and fell ill. This was three months ago, and then there was absolutely no food at all. They made no complaint, spoke no word; but poor folk know. The housewives of Batavia Road sent them food, but so respectable were the Cavillas that the food was sent anonymously, mysteriously, so as not to hurt their pride.

The thing had happened. He had fought, and starved, and suffered for eighteen months. He got up one September morning, early. He opened his pocket-knife. He cut the throat of his wife, Hannah Cavilla, aged thirty-three. He cut the throat of his first-born, Frank, aged twelve. He cut the throat of his son, Walter, aged eight. He cut the throat of his daughter, Nellie, aged four. He cut the throat of his youngest-born, Ernest, aged sixteen months. Then he watched beside the dead all day until the evening, when the police came, and he told them to put a penny in the slot of the gas-meter in order that they might have light to see.

Frank Cavilla stood in court, dressed in a much worn grey suit, and wearing no collar. He was a good-looking man, with a mass of black hair, dark, expressive eyes, delicately chiselled nose and chin, and wavy, fair moustache.

CHAPTER TWENTY-THREE

THE CHILDREN

'Where home is a hovel, and dull we grovel,
Forgetting the world is fair.'

THERE is one beautiful sight in the East End, and only one, and it is the children dancing in the street when the organ-grinder goes his round. It is fascinating to watch them, the new-born, the next generation, swaying and stepping, with pretty little mimicries and graceful inventions all their own, with muscles that move swiftly and easily, and bodies that leap airily, weaving rhythms never taught in dancing school.

I have talked with these children, here, there, and everywhere, and they struck me as being bright as other children, and in many ways even brighter. They have most active little imaginations. Their capacity for projecting themselves into the realm of romance and fantasy is remarkable. A joyous life is romping in their blood. They delight in music, and motion, and colour, and very often they betray a startling beauty of face and form under their filth and rags.

But there is a Pied Piper of London Town who steals them all away. They disappear. One never sees them again, or anything that suggests them. You may look for them in vain amongst the generation of grown-ups. Here you will find stunted forms, ugly faces, and blunt and stolid minds. Grace, beauty, imagination, all the resiliency of mind and muscle, are gone. Sometimes, however, you may see a woman, not necessarily old, but twisted and deformed out of all womanhood, bloated and drunken, lift her draggled skirts and execute a few grotesque and lumbering steps upon the pavement. It is a hint that she was once one of those children who danced to the organ-grinder. Those grotesque and lumbering steps are all that is left of the promise of childhood. In the befogged recesses of her brain has arisen a fleeting memory that she was once a girl. The crowd closes in. Little girls are dancing beside her, about her, with all the pretty graces she dimly recollects, but can no more than parody with her body. Then she pants for breath, exhausted, and stumbles out through the circle. But the little girls dance on.

The children of the Ghetto possess all the qualities which make for noble-manhood and womanhood, but the Ghetto itself, like an infuriated tigress turning on its young, turns upon and destroys all these qualities, blots out the light and laughter, and moulds those it does not kill into sodden and forlorn creatures, uncouth, degraded, and wretched below the beasts of the field.

As to the manner in which this is done, I have in previous chapters described it at length; here let Professor Huxley describe it in brief:

'Any one who is acquainted with the state of the population of all great industrial centres, whether in this or other countries, is aware that amidst a large and increasing body of that population there reigns supreme ... that condition which the French call *la misère*, a word for which I do not think there is any exact English equivalent. It is a condition in which the food, warmth, and clothing which are necessary for the mere maintenance of the functions of the body in their normal state cannot be obtained; in which men, women, and children are forced to crowd into dens wherein decency is abolished, and the most ordinary conditions of healthful existence are impossible of attainment; in which the pleasures within reach are reduced to brutality and drunkenness; in which the pains accumulate at compound interest in the shape of starvation, disease, stunted development, and moral degradation; in which the prospect of even steady and honest industry is a life of unsuccessful battling with hunger, rounded by a pauper's grave.'

In such conditions, the outlook for children is hopeless. They die like flies, and those that survive, survive because they possess excessive vitality and a capacity of adaptation to the degradation with which they are surrounded. They have no home life. In the dens and lairs in which they live they are exposed to all that is obscene and indecent. And as their minds are made rotten, so are their bodies made rotten by bad sanitation, overcrowding, and underfeeding. When a father and mother live with three or four children in a room where the children take turn about in sitting up to drive the rats away from the sleepers, when those children never have enough to eat and are preyed upon and made miserable and weak by swarming vermin, the sort of men and women the survivors will make can readily be imagined.

> *Dull despair and misery*
> *Lie about them from their birth;*
> *Ugly curses, uglier mirth,*
> *Are their earliest lullaby.'*

A man and a woman marry and set up housekeeping in one room. Their income does not increase with the years, though their family does, and the man is exceedingly lucky if he can keep his health and his job. A baby comes, and then another. This means that more room should be obtained; but these little mouths and bodies mean additional expense and make it absolutely impossible to get more spacious quarters. More babies come. There is not room in which to turn around. The youngsters run the streets, and by the time they are twelve or fourteen the room-issue comes to a head, and out they go on the streets for good. The boy, if he be lucky, can manage to make the common lodging-houses, and he may have any one of several ends. But the girl of fourteen or fifteen, forced in this manner to leave the one room called home, and able to earn at the best a paltry five or six shillings per week, can have but one end. And the bitter end of that one end is such as that of the woman whose body the police found this morning in a doorway in Dorset Street, Whitechapel. Homeless, shelterless, sick, with no one with her in her last hour, she had died in the night of exposure. She was sixty-two years old and a match vendor. She died as a wild animal dies.

Fresh in my mind is the picture of a boy in the dock of an East End police court. His head was barely visible above the railing. He was being proved guilty of stealing two shillings from a woman, which he had spent, not for candy and cakes and a good time, but for food.

'Why didn't you ask the woman for food?' the magistrate demanded, in a hurt sort of tone. 'She would surely have given you something to eat.'

'If I 'ad arsked 'er, I'd got locked up for beggin',' was the boy's reply.

The magistrate knitted his brows and accepted the rebuke. Nobody knew the boy, nor his father or mother. He was without beginning or antecedent, a waif, a stray, a young cub seeking his food in the jungle of empire, preying upon the weak and being preyed upon by the strong.

The people who try to help, who gather up the Ghetto children and send them away on a day's outing to the country, believe that not very many children reach the age of ten without having had a least one day there. Of this, a writer says: 'The mental change caused by one day so spent must not be undervalued. Whatever the circumstances, the children learn the meaning of fields and woods, so that descriptions of country scenery in the books they read, which before conveyed no impression, become now intelligible.'

One day in the fields and woods, if they are lucky enough to be picked up by the people who try to help! And they are being born faster every day than they can be carted off to the fields and woods for the one day in their lives. One day! In all their lives, one day! And for the rest of the days, as the boy told a certain bishop, 'At ten we 'ops the wag; at thirteen we nicks things; an' at sixteen we bashes the copper.' Which is to say, at ten they play truant, at thirteen steal, and at sixteen are sufficiently developed hooligans to smash the policemen.

The Rev. J. Cartmel Robinson tells of a boy and girl of his parish who set out to walk to the forest. They walked and walked through the never-ending streets, expecting always to see it by-and-by; until they sat down at last, faint and despairing, and were rescued by a kind woman who brought them back. Evidently they had been overlooked by the people who try to help.

The same gentleman is authority for the statement that in a street in Hoxton (a district of the vast East End), over seven hundred children, between five and thirteen years live in eighty small houses. And he adds: 'It is because London has largely shut her children in a maze of streets and houses and robbed them of their rightful inheritance in sky and field and brook, that they grow up to be men and women physically unfit.'

He tells of a member of his congregation who let a basement room to a married couple. 'They said they had two children; when they got possession it turned out that they had four. After a while a fifth appeared, and the landlord gave them notice to quit. They paid no attention to it. Then the sanitary inspector, who has to wink at the law so often, came in and threatened my friend with legal proceedings. He pleaded that he could not get them out. They pleaded that nobody would have them with so many children at a rental within their means, which is one of the commonest complaints of the poor, by-the-bye. What was to be done? The landlord was between two millstones. Finally he applied to the magistrate, who sent up an officer to inquire into the case. Since that time about twenty days have elapsed, and nothing has yet been done. Is this a singular case? By no means; it is quite common.'

Last week the police raided a disorderly house. In one room were found two young children. They were arrested and charged with being inmates the same as the women had been. Their father appeared at the trial. He stated that himself and wife and two older children, besides the two in the dock, occupied that room; he stated also that he occupied it because he could get no other room for the half-crown a week he paid for it. The magistrate discharged the two juvenile offenders and warned the father that he was bringing his children up unhealthily.

But there is no need further to multiply instances. In London the slaughter of the innocents goes on on a scale more stupendous than any before in the history of the world. And equally stupendous is the callousness of the people who believe in Christ, acknowledge God, and go to church regularly on Sunday. For the rest of the week they riot about on the rents and profits which come to them from the East End stained with the blood of the children. Also, at times, so peculiarly are they made, they will take half a million of these rents and profits and send it away to educate the black boys of the Soudan.

CHAPTER TWENTY-FOUR

A VISION OF THE NIGHT

All these were years ago little red-coloured, pulpy infants, capable of being kneaded, baked, into any social form you chose. – CARLYLE

LATE last night I walked along Commercial Street from Spitalfields to Whitechapel, and still continuing south, down Leman Street to the docks. And as I walked I smiled at the East End papers, which, filled with civic pride, boastfully proclaim that there is nothing the matter with the East End as a living place for men and women.

It is rather hard to tell a tithe of what I saw. Much of it is untellable. But in a general way I may say that I saw a nightmare, a fearful slime that quickened the pavement with life, a mess of unmentionable obscenity that put into eclipse the 'nightly horror' of Piccadilly and the Strand. It was a menagerie of garmented bipeds that looked something like humans and more like beasts, and to complete the picture, brass-buttoned keepers kept order among them when they snarled too fiercely.

I was glad the keepers were there, for I did not have on my 'Seafaring' clothes, and I was what is called a 'mark' for the creatures of prey that prowled up and down. At times, between keepers, these males looked at me, sharply, hungrily, gutter-wolves that they were, and I was afraid of their hands, of their naked hands, as one may be afraid of the paws of a gorilla. They reminded me of gorillas. Their bodies were small, ill-shaped, and squat. There were no swelling muscles, no abundant thews and wide-spreading shoulders. They exhibited, rather, an elemental economy of nature, such as the cave-men must have exhibited. But there was strength in those meagre bodies, the ferocious primordial strength to clutch and gripe and tear and rend. When they spring upon their human prey they are known even to bend the victim backward and double its body till the back is broken. They possess neither conscience or sentiment, and they will kill for a half-sovereign, without fear or favour, if they are given but half a chance. They are a new species, a breed of city savages. The streets and houses, alleys and courts, are their hunting grounds. As valley and mountain are to the natural savage, street and building are valley and mountain to them. The slum is their jungle, and they live and prey in the jungle.

The dear soft people of the golden theatres and wonder-mansions of the West End do not see these creatures, do not dream that they exist. But they are here, alive, very much alive in their jungle. And woe the day, when England is fighting in her last trench, and her able-bodied men are on the firing line! For on that day they will crawl out of their dens and lairs, and the people of the West End will see them, as the dear soft aristocrats of Feudal France saw them and asked one another, 'whence came they?' 'Are they men?'

But they were not the only beasts that ranged the menagerie. They were only here and there, lurking in dark courts and passing like grey shadows along the walls; but the women from whose rotten loins they spring were everywhere. They whined insolently, and in maudlin tones begged me for pennies, and worse. They held carouse in every boozing ken, slatternly, unkempt, bleary-eyed, and towsled, leering and gibbering, overspilling with foulness and corruption, and gone in debauch, sprawling across benches and bars, unspeakably repulsive, fearful to look upon.

And there were others, strange, weird faces and forms and twisted monstrosities, that shouldered me on every side, inconceivable types of sodden ugliness, the wrecks of society, the perambulating carcasses, the living deaths – women, blasted by disease and drink till their shame brought not tuppence in the open mart; and men, in fantastic rags, wrenched by hardship and exposure out of all semblance of men, their faces in a perpetual writhe of pain, grinning idiotically, shambling like apes, dying with every step they took and each breath they drew. And there were young girls, of eighteen and twenty, with trim bodies and faces yet untouched with twist and bloat, who had fetched the bottom of the abyss plump, in one swift fall. And I remember a lad of fourteen, and one of six or seven, white-faced and sickly, homeless, the pair of them, who sat upon the pavement with their backs against a railing and watched it all.

The unfit and the unneeded! Industry does not clamour for them. There are no jobs going begging through lack of men and women. The dockers crowd at the entrance gate, and curse, and turn away when the foreman does not give them a call. The engineers who have work pay six shillings a week to their brother engineers who can find nothing to do; 514,000 textile workers oppose a resolution condemning the employment of children under fifteen. Women, and plenty to spare, are found to toil under the sweat-shop masters for tenpence a day of fourteen hours. Alfred Freeman crawls to muddy death because he loses his job. Ellen Hughes Hunt prefers Regent's Canal to Islington Workhouse. Frank Cavilla cuts the throats of his wife and children, because he cannot find work enough to give them food and shelter.

The unfit and the unneeded! The miserable and despised and forgotten, dying in the social shambles. The progeny of prostitution – of the prostitution of men and women and children, of flesh and blood, and sparkle and spirit; in brief, the prostitution of labour. if this is the best that civilization can do for the human, then give us howling and naked savagery. Far better to be a people of the wilderness and desert, of the cave and the squatting-place, than to be a people of the machine and the Abyss.

CHAPTER TWENTY-FIVE

THE HUNGER WAIL

'My father has more stamina than I, for he is country-born.'

The speaker, a bright young East Ender, was lamenting his poor physical development.

'Look at my scrawny arm, will you.' He pulled up his sleeve. 'Not enough to eat, that's what's the matter with it. Oh, not now. I have what I want to eat these days. But it's too late. It can't make up for what I didn't have to eat when I was a kiddy. Dad came up to London from the Fen Country. Mother died, and there were six of us kiddies and dad living in two small rooms.

'He had hard times, dad did. He might have chucked us, but he didn't. He slaved all day, and at night he came home and cooked and cared for us. He was father and mother, both. He did his best, but we didn't have enough to eat. We rarely saw meat, and then of the worst. And it is not good for growing kiddies to sit down to a dinner of bread and a bit of cheese, and not enough of it.

'And what's the result? I am undersized, and I haven't the stamina of my dad. It was starved out of me. In a couple of generations there'll be no more of me here in London. Yet there's my younger brother; he's bigger and better developed. You see, dad and we children held together, and that accounts for it.'

'But I don't see,' I objected. 'I should think, under such conditions, that the vitality should decrease and the younger children be born weaker and weaker.'

'Not when they hold together,' he replied. 'Whenever you come along in the East End and see a child of from eight to twelve, good-sized, well-developed, and healthy-looking, just you ask and you will find that it is the youngest in the family, or at least is one of the younger. The way of it is this: the older children starve more than the younger ones. By the time the younger ones come along, the older ones are starting to work, and there is more money coming in, and more food to go around.'

He pulled down his sleeve, a concrete instance of where chronic semi-starvation kills not, but stunts. His voice was but one among the myriads that raise the cry of the hunger wail in the greatest empire in the world. On any one day, over 1,000,000 people are in receipt of poor-law relief in the United Kingdom. One in eleven of the whole working-class receive poor-law relief in the course of the year; 37,500,000 people receive less than £12 per month, per family; and a constant army of 8,000,000 lives on the border of starvation.

A committee of the London County school board makes this declaration: 'At times, *when there is no special distress*, 55,000 children in a state of hunger, which makes it useless to attempt to teach them, are in the schools of London alone.' The italics are mine. 'When there is no special distress' means good times in England; for the people of England have come to look upon starvation and suffering, which they call 'distress', as part of the social order. Chronic starvation is looked upon as a matter of course. It is only when acute starvation makes its appearance on a large scale that they think something is unusual.

I shall never forget the bitter wail of a blind man in a little East End shop at the close of a murky day. He had been the eldest of five children, with a mother and no father. Being the eldest, he had starved and worked as a child to put bread into the mouths of his little brothers and sisters. Not once in three months did he ever taste meat. He never knew what it was to have his hunger thoroughly appeased. And he claimed that this chronic starvation of his child-hood had robbed him of his sight. To support the claim, he quoted from the report of the Royal Commission on the Blind, 'Blindness is most prevalent in poor districts, and poverty accelerates this dreadful affliction.'

But he went further, this blind man, and in his voice was the bitterness of an afflicted man to whom society did not give enough to eat. He was one of an enormous army of blind in London, and he said that in the blind homes they did not receive half enough to eat. He gave the diet for a day:

Breakfast—½ pint of skilly and dry bread.
Dinner—3 oz. meat.
1 slice of bread.
½ lb. potatoes.
Supper—½ pint of skilly and dry bread.

Oscar Wilde, God rest his soul, voices the cry of the prison child, which, in varying degree, is the cry of the prison man and woman: 'The second thing from which a child suffers in prison is hunger. The food that is given to it consists of a piece of usually bad-baked prison bread and a tin of water for breakfast at half-past seven. At twelve o'clock it gets dinner, composed of a tin of coarse Indian meal stirabout (skilly), and at half-past five it gets a piece of dry bread and a tin of water for its supper. This diet in the case of a strong grown man is always productive of illness of some kind, chiefly of course diarrhoea, with its attendant weakness. In fact, in a big prison astringent medicines are served out regularly by the warders as a matter of course. In the case of a child, the child is, as a rule, incapable of eating the food at all. Any one who knows anything about children knows how easily a child's digestion is upset by a fit of crying, or trouble and mental distress of any kind. A child who has been crying all day long, and perhaps half the night, in a lonely dim-lit cell, and is preyed upon by terror, simply cannot eat food of this coarse, horrible kind. In the case of the little child to whom Warder Martin gave the biscuits, the child was crying with hunger on Tuesday morning, and utterly unable to eat the bread and water served to it for its breakfast. Martin went out after the breakfasts had been served and bought the few sweet biscuits for the child rather than see it starving. It was a beautiful action on his part, and was so recognized by the child, who, utterly unconscious of the regulations of the Prison Board, told one of the senior wardens how kind this junior warden had been to him. The result was, of course, a report and a dismissal.'

Robert Blatchford compares the workhouse pauper's daily diet with the soldier's, which, when he was a soldier, was not considered liberal enough, and yet is twice as liberal as the pauper's.

PAUPER	DIET	SOLDIER
3¼ oz.	Meat	12 oz.
15½ oz.	Bread	24 oz.
6 oz.	Vegetables	8 oz.

The adult male pauper gets meat (outside of soup) but once a week, and the paupers 'have nearly all that pallid, pasty complexion which is the sure mark of starvation.'

Here is a table, comparing the workhouse pauper's weekly allowance with the workhouse officer's weekly allowance:

OFFICER	DIET	PAUPER
7 lb.	Bread	6¾ lb.
5 lb.	Meat	1 lb. 2 oz.
12 oz.	Bacon	2½ oz.
8 oz.	Cheese	2 oz.
7 lb.	Potatoes	1½ lb.
6 lb.	Vegetables	none
1 lb.	Flour	none
2 oz.	Lard	none
12 oz.	Butter	7 oz.
none	Rice pudding	1 lb.

And as the same writer remarks: 'The officer's diet is still more liberal than the pauper's; but evidently it is not considered liberal enough, for a footnote is added to the officer's table saying that 'a cash payment of two shillings and sixpence a week is also made to each resident officer and servant.' If the pauper has ample food, why does the officer have more? And if the officer has not too much, can the pauper be properly fed on less than half the amount?

But it is not alone the Ghetto-dweller, the prisoner, and the pauper that starve. Hodge, of the country, does not know what it is always to have a full belly. In truth, it is his empty belly which has driven him to the city in such great numbers. Let us investigate the way of living of a labourer from a parish in the Bradfield Poor Law Union, Berks. Supposing him to have two children, steady work, a rent-free cottage, and an average weekly wage of about thirteen shillings, which is equivalent to $3.25, then here is his weekly budget:

		s	d
Bread (5 quarterns)	. . . . .	1	10
Flour (½ gallon)	. . . . .		4
Tea (¼ lb.)	. . . . .		6
Butter (1 lb.)	. . . . .	1	3
Lard (1 lb.)	. . . . .		6
Sugar (6 lb.)	. . . . .	1	0
Bacon or other meat (about 4 lb.)	. .	2	8
Cheese (1 lb.)	. . . . .		8
Milk (half-tin condensed)	. . .		3¼
Oil, candles, blue, soap, salt, pepper, &c.	.	1	0
Coal	. . . . .	1	6
Beer	. . . . .		none
Tobacco	. . . . .		none

						s	d
Insurance (' Prudential ')	.	.	.	.			3
Labourers' Union .	.	.	.	.			1
Wood, tools, dispensary, &c.	.	.	.				6
Insurance (' Foresters ') and margin for clothes	.					1	1¾
Total	.	.	.	.	.	13	6

The guardians of the workhouse in the above Union pride themselves on their rigid economy. It costs per pauper per week:

						s	d
Men .	.	.	.	.	.	6	1½
Women	.	.	.	.	.	5	6½
Children	.	.	.	.	.	5	1¼

If the labourer whose budget has been described should quit his toil and go into the workhouse, he would cost the guardians for

						s	d
Himself	.	.	.	.	.	6	1½
Wife	.	.	.	.	.	5	6½
Two children	.	.	.	.	.	10	2½
Total	.	.	.	.	.	21	10½

Or roughly, $5.46

It would require more than a guinea for the workhouse to care for him and his family, which he, somehow, manages to do on thirteen shillings. And, in addition, it is an understood fact that it is cheaper to cater for a large number of people – buying, cooking, and serving wholesale – than it is to cater for a small number of people, say a family.

Nevertheless, at the time this budget was compiled, there was in that parish, another family, not of four, but *eleven* persons, who had to live on an income, not of thirteen shillings, but of twelve shillings per week (eleven shillings in winter), and which had, not a rent-free cottage, but a cottage for which it paid three shillings per week.

This must be understood, and understood clearly: *Whatever is true of London in the way of poverty and degradation, is true of all England.* While Paris is not by any means France, the city of London is England. The frightful conditions which mark London an inferno likewise mark the United Kingdom an inferno. The argument that the decentralization of London would ameliorate conditions is a vain thing and false. If the 6,000,000 people of London were separated into one hundred cities each with a population of 60,000, misery would be decentralized but not diminished. The sum of it would remain as large.

In this instance, Mr. B. S. Rowntree, by an exhaustive analysis, has proved for the country town what Mr. Charles Booth has proved for the metropolis, that fully one-fourth of the dwellers are condemned to a poverty which destroys them physically and spiritually; that fully one-fourth of the dwellers do not have enough to eat, are inadequately clothed, sheltered, and warmed in a rigorous climate, and are doomed to a moral degeneracy which puts them lower than the savage in cleanliness and decency.

After listening to the wail of an old Irish peasant in Kerry, Robert Blatchford asked him what he wanted. 'The old man leaned upon his spade and looked out across the black peat fields at the lowering skies. "What is it that I'm wantun?" he said; then in a deep plaintive tone he continued, more to himself than to me, "All our brave bhoys and dear gurlls is away an' over the says, an' the agent has taken the pig off me, an' the wet has spiled the praties, an' I'm an owled man, *an' I want the Day av Judgment*." '

The Day of Judgment! More than he want it. From all the land rises the hunger wail, from Ghetto and countryside, from prison and casual ward, from asylum and workhouse – the cry of the people who have not enough to eat. Millions of people, men, women, children, the little babes, the blind, the deaf, the halt, the sick, vagabonds and toilers, prisoners and paupers, the people of Ireland, England, Scotland, Wales, who have not enough to eat. And this, in face of the fact that five men can produce bread for a thousand; that one workman can produce cotton cloth for 250 people, woollens for 300, and boots and shoes for 1,000. It would seem that 40,000,000 people are keeping a big house, and that they are keeping it badly. The income is all right, but there is something criminally wrong with the management. And who dares to say that it is not criminally mismanaged, this big house, when five men can produce bread for a thousand, and yet millions have not enough to eat?

CHAPTER TWENTY-SIX

DRINK, TEMPERANCE AND THRIFT

THE English working classes may be said to be soaked in beer. They are made dull and sodden by it. Their efficiency is sadly impaired, and they lose whatever imagination, invention, and quickness may be theirs by right of race. It may hardly be called an acquired habit, for they are accustomed to it from their earliest infancy. Children are begotten in drunkenness, saturated in drink before they draw their first breath, born to the smell and taste of it, and brought up in the midst of it.

The public-house is ubiquitous. It flourishes on every corner and between corners, and it is frequented almost as much by women as by men. Children are to be found in it as well, waiting till their fathers and mothers are ready to go home, sipping from the glasses of their elders, listening to the coarse language and degrading conversation, catching the contagion of it, familiarizing themselves with licentiousness and debauchery.

Mrs. Grundy rules as supremely over the workers as she does over the bourgeoisie; but in the case of the workers, the one thing she does not frown upon is the public-house. No disgrace or shame attaches to it, nor to the young woman or girl who makes a practice of entering it.

I remember a girl in a coffee-house saying, 'I never drink spirits when in a public-'ouse.' She was a young and pretty waitress, and she was laying down to another waitress her pre-eminent respectability and discretion. Mrs. Grundy drew the line at spirits, but allowed that it was quite proper for a clean young girl to drink beer, and to go into a public-house to drink it.

Not only is this beer unfit for the people to drink, but too often the men and women are unfit to drink it. On the other hand, it is their very unfitness that drives them to drink it. Ill-fed, suffering from innutrition, and the evil effects of overcrowding and squalor, their constitutions develop a morbid craving for the drink, just as the sickly stomach of the overstrung Manchester factory operative hankers after excessive quantities of pickles and similar weird foods. Unhealthy working and living engenders unhealthy appetites and desires. Man cannot be worked worse than a horse is worked, and be housed and fed as a pig is housed and fed, and at the same time have clean and wholesome ideals and aspirations.

As home-life vanishes, the public-house appears. Not only do men and women abnormally crave drink, who are overworked, exhausted, suffering from deranged stomachs and bad sanitation, and deadened by the ugliness and monotony of existence, but the gregarious men and women who have no home-life flee to the bright and clattering public-house in a vain attempt to express their gregariousness. And when a family is housed in one small room, home-life is impossible.

A brief examination of such a dwelling will serve to bring to light one important cause of drunkenness. Here the family arises in the morning, dresses, and makes its toilet, father, mother, sons, and daughters, and in the same room, shoulder to shoulder (for the room is small), the wife and mother cooks the breakfast. And the same room, heavy and sickening with the exhalations of their packed bodies throughout the night, that breakfast is eaten. The father goes to work, the elder children go to school or into the street, and the mother remains with her crawling, toddling youngsters to do her housework – still in the same room. Here she washes the clothes, filling the pent space with soapsuds and the smell of dirty clothes, and overhead she hangs the wet linen to dry.

Here, in the evening, amid the manifold smells of the day, the family goes to its virtuous couch. That is to say, as many as possible pile into the one bed (if bed they have), and the surplus turns in on the floor. And this is the round of their existence, month after month, year after year, for they never get a vacation save when they are evicted. When a child dies, and some are always bound to die, since fifty-five per cent of the East End children die before they are five years old, the body is laid out in the same room. And if they are

121

very poor, it is kept for some time until they can bury it. During the day it lies on the bed; during the night when the living take the bed, the dead occupies the table, from which, in the morning, when the dead is put back into the bed, they eat their breakfast. Sometimes the body is placed on the shelf which serves as a pantry for their food. Only a couple of weeks ago, an East End woman was in trouble, because, in this fashion, being unable to bury it, she had kept her dead child three weeks.

Now such a room as I have described is not home but horror; and the men and women who flee away from it to the public-house are to be pitied, not blamed. There are 300,000 people, in London, divided into families that live in single rooms, while there are 900,000 who are illegally housed according to the Public Health Act of 1891 – a respectable recruiting-ground for the drink traffic.

Then there are the insecurity of happiness, the precariousness of existence, the well-founded fear of the future – potent factors in driving people to drink. Wretchedness squirms for alleviation, and in the public-house its pain is eased and forgetfulness is obtained. It is unhealthy. Certainly it is, but everything else about their lives is unhealthy, while this brings the oblivion that nothing else in their lives can bring. It even exalts them, and makes them feel that they are finer and better, though at the same time it drags them down and makes them more beastly than ever. For the unfortunate man or woman, it is a race between miseries that ends with death.

It is of no avail to preach temperance and teetotalism to these people. The drink habit may be the cause of many miseries; but it is, in turn, the effect of other and prior miseries. The temperance advocates may preach their hearts out over the evils of drink, but until the evils that cause people to drink are abolished, drink and its evils will remain.

Until the people who try to help realize this, their well-intentioned efforts will be futile, and they will present a spectacle fit only to set Olympus laughing. I have gone through an exhibition of Japanese art, got up for the poor of Whitechapel with the idea of elevating them, of begetting in them yearnings for the Beautiful and True and Good. Granting (what is not so) that the poor folk are thus taught to know and yearn after the Beautiful and True and Good, the foul facts of their existence and the social law that dooms one in three to a public-charity death, demonstrate that this knowledge and yearning will be only so much of an added curse to them. They will have so much more to forget than if they had never known and yearned. Did Destiny today bind me down to the life of an East End slave for the rest of my years, and did Destiny grant me but one wish, I should ask that I might forget all about the Beautiful and True and Good; that I might forget all I had learned from the open books, and forget the people I had known, the things I had heard, and the lands I had seen. And if Destiny didn't grant it, I am pretty confident that I should get drunk and forget it as often as possible.

These people who try to help! Their college settlements, missions, charities, and what not, are failures. In the nature of things they cannot but be failures. They are wrongly, though sincerely, conceived. They approach life through a misunderstanding of life, these good folk. They do not understand the West End, yet they come down to the East End as teachers and savants. They do not understand the simply sociology of Christ, yet they come to the miserable and the despised with the pomp of social redeemers. They have worked faithfully, but beyond relieving an infinitesimal fraction of misery and collecting a certain amount of data, which might otherwise have been more scientifically and less expensively collected, they have achieved nothing.

As someone has said, they do everything for the poor except get off their backs. The very money they dribble out in their child's schemes has been wrung from the poor. They come from a race of successful and predatory bipeds who stand between the worker and his wages, and they try to tell the worker what he shall do with the pitiful balance left to him. Of what use, in the name of God, is it to establish nurseries for women workers, in which, for instance, a child is taken while the mother makes violets in Islington at three farthings a gross, when more children and violet-makers than they can cope with are being born right along? This violet-maker handles each flower four times, 576 handlings for three farthings, and in the day she handles the flowers 6,912 times for a wage of ninepence. She is being robbed. Somebody is on her back, and a yearning for the Beautiful and True and Good will not lighten her burden. They do nothing for her, these dabblers; and what they do not do for the mother, undoes at night, when the child comes home, all that they have done for the child in the day.

And one and all, they join in teaching a fundamental lie. They do not know it is a lie, but their ignorance does not make it more of a truth. And the lie they preach is 'thrift'. An instant will demonstrate it. In overcrowded London, the struggle for a chance to work is keen, and because of this struggle wages sink to the lowest means of subsistence. To be thrifty means for a worker to spend less than his income – in other words, to live on less. This is equivalent to a lowering of the standard of living. In the competition for a chance to work, the man with a lower standard of living will underbid the man with a higher standard. And a small group of such thrifty workers in any overcrowded industry will permanently lower the wages of that industry. And the thrifty ones will no longer be thrifty, for their income will have been reduced till it balances their expenditure.

In short, thrift negates thrift. If every worker in England should heed the preachers of thrift and cut expenditure in half, the condition of there being more men to work than there is work to do would swiftly cut wages in half. And then none of the workers of England would be thrifty, for they would be living up to their diminished incomes. The short-sighted thrift-preachers would naturally be astounded at the outcome. The measure of their failure would be precisely the measure of the success of the propaganda. And, anyway, it is sheer bosh and nonesense to preach thrift to the 1,800,000 London workers who are divided into families which have a total income of less than 21s. per week, one quarter to one half of which must be paid for rent.

Concerning the futility of the people who try to help, I wish to make one notable, noble exception, namely, the Dr. Barnardo Homes. Dr. Barnardo is a child-catcher. First, he catches them when they are young, before they are set, hardened, in the vicious social mould; and then he sends them away to grow up and be formed in another and better social mould. Up to date he has sent out of the country 13,340 boys, most of them to Canada, and not one in fifty has failed. A splendid record, when it is considered that these lads are waifs and strays, homeless and parentless, jerked out from the very bottom of the Abyss, and forty-nine out of fifty of them made into men.

Every twenty-four hours in the year Dr. Barnardo snatches nine waifs from the streets; so the enormous field he has to work in may be comprehended. The people who try to help have something to learn from him. He does not play with palliatives. He traces social viciousness and misery to their sources. He removes the progeny of the gutter-folk from their pestilential environment, and gives them a healthy, wholesome environment in which to be pressed and prodded and moulded into men.

When the people who try to help cease their playing and dabbling with day nurseries and Japanese art exhibits and go back and learn their West End and the sociology of Christ, they will be in better shape to buckle down to the work they ought to be doing in the world. And if they do buckle down to the work, they will follow Dr. Barnardo's lead, only on a scale as large as the nation is large. They won't cram yearnings for the Beautiful, and True, and Good down the throat of the woman making violets for three farthings a gross, but they will make somebody get off her back and quit cramming himself till, like the Romans, he must go to a bath and sweat it out. And to their consternation, they will find that they will have to get off that woman's back themselves, as well as the backs of a few other women and children they did not dream they were riding upon.

CHAPTER TWENTY-SEVEN

THE MANAGEMENT

In this final chapter it were well to look at the Social Abyss in its widest aspect, and to put certain questions to Civilization, by the answers to which Civilization must stand or fall. For instance, has Civilization bettered the lot of man? 'Man', I use in its democratic sense, meaning the average man. So the question re-shapes itself: *Has Civilization bettered the lot of the average man?*

Let us see. In Alaska, along the banks of the Yukon River, near its mouth, live the Innuit folk. They are a very primitive people, manifesting but mere glimmering adumbrations of that tremendous artifice, Civilization. Their capital amounts possibly to £2 per head. They hunt and fish for their food with bone-headed spears and arrows. They never suffer from lack of shelter. Their clothes largely made from the skins of animals, are warm. They always have fuel for their fires, likewise timber for their houses, which they build partly underground, and in which they lie snugly during the periods of intense cold. In the summer they live in tents, open to every breeze and cool. They are healthy, and strong, and happy. Their one problem is food. They have their times of plenty and times of famine. In good times they feast; in bad times they die of starvation. But starvation, as a chronic condition, present with a large number of them all the time, is a thing unknown. Further, they have no debts.

In the United Kingdom, on the rim of the Western Ocean, live the English folk. They are a consummately civilized people. Their capital amounts to at least £300 per head. They gain their food, not by hunting and fishing, but by toil at colossal artifices. For the most part, they suffer from lack of shelter. The greater number of them are vilely housed, do not have enough fuel to keep them warm, and are insufficiently clothed. A constant number never have any houses at all, and sleep shelterless under the stars. Many are to be found, winter and summer, shivering on the streets in their rags. They have good times and bad. In good times most of them manage to get enough to eat, in bad times they die of starvation. They are dying now, they were dying yesterday and last year, they will die tomorrow and next year, of starvation; for they, unlike the Innuit, suffer from a chronic condition of starvation. There are 40,000,000 of the English folk, and 939 out of every 1,000 of them die in poverty, while a constant army of 8,000,000 struggles on the ragged edge of starvation. Further, each babe that is born, is born in debt to the sum of £22. This is because of an artifice called the National Debt.

In a fair comparison of the average Innuit and the average Englishman, it will be seen that life is less rigorous for the Innuit; that while the Innuit suffers only during the bad times from starvation, the Englishman suffers during good times as well; that no Innuit lacks fuel, clothing, or housing, while the Englishman is in perpetual lack of these three essentials. In this connection it is well to instance the judgment of a man such as Huxley. From the knowledge gained as a medical officer in the East End of London, and as a scientist pursuing investigations among the most elemental savages, he concludes, 'Were the alternative presented to me, I would deliberately prefer the life of the savage to that of those people of Christian London.'

The creature comforts man enjoys are the products of man's labour. Since Civilization has failed to give the average Englishman food and shelter equal to that enjoyed by the Innuit, the question arises: *Has Civilization increased the producing power of the average man?* If it has not increased man's producing power, then Civilization cannot stand.

But, it will be instantly admitted, Civilization *has* increased man's producing power. Five men can produce bread for a thousand. One man can produce cotton cloth for 250 people, woollens for 300, and boots and shoes for 1,000. Yet it has been shown throughout the pages of this book that English folk by the millions do not receive enough food, clothes, and boots. Then arises the third and inexorable question: *If Civilization has increased the producing power of the average man, why has it not bettered the lot of the average man?*

There can be one answer only – MISMANAGEMENT. Civilization has made possible all manner of creature comforts and heart's delights. In these the average Englishman does not participate. If he shall be forever unable to participate, then Civilization falls. There is no reason for the continued existence of an artifice so avowed a failure. But it is impossible that men should have reared this tremendous artifice in vain. It stuns the intellect. To acknowledge so crushing a defeat is to give the death-blow to striving and progress.

One other alternative, and one other only, presents itself. *Civilization must be compelled to better the lot of the average man.* This accepted, it becomes at once a question of business management. Things profitable must be continued; things unprofitable must be eliminated. Either the Empire is a profit to England, or it is a loss. If it is a loss, it must be done away with. If it is a profit, it must be managed so that the average man comes in for a share of the profit.

If the struggle for commercial supremacy is profitable, continue it. If it is not, if it hurts the worker and makes his lot worse than the lot of a savage, then fling foreign markets and industrial empire overboard. For it is a patent fact that if 40,000,000 people, aided by Civilization, possess a greater individual producing power than the Innuit, then those 40,000,000 people should enjoy more creature comforts and heart's delights than the Innuits enjoy.

If the 400,000 English gentlemen, 'of no occupation', according to their own statement in the Census of 1881, are unprofitable, do away with them. Set them to work ploughing game preserves and planting potatoes. If they are profitable, continue them by all means, but let it be seen to that the average Englishman shares somewhat in the profits they produce by working at no occupation.

In short, society must be reorganized, and a capable management put at the head. That the present management is incapable, there can be no discussion. It has drained the United Kingdom of its life-blood. It has enfeebled the stay-at-home folk till they are unable longer to struggle in the van of the competing nations. It has built up a West End and an East End as large as the Kingdom is large, in which one end is riotous and rotten, the other end sickly and underfed.

A vast empire is foundering on the hands of this incapable

management. And by empire is meant the political machinery which holds together the English-speaking people of the world outside of the United States. Nor is this charged in a pessimistic spirit. Blood empire is greater than political empire, and the English of the New World and the Antipodes are strong and vigorous as ever. But the political empire under which they are nominally assembled is perishing. The political machine known as the British Empire is running down. In the hands of its management it is losing momentum every day.

It is inevitable that this management, which has grossly and criminally mismanaged, shall be swept away. Not only has it been wasteful and inefficient, but it has misappropriated the funds. Every worn-out, pasty-faced pauper, every blind man, every prison babe, every man, woman, and child whose belly is gnawing with hunger pangs, is hungry because the funds have been misappropriated by the management.

Nor can one member of this managing class plead not guilty before the judgment bar of Man. 'The living in their houses, and in their graves the dead', are challenged by every babe that dies of innutrition, by every girl that flees the sweater's den to the nightly promenade of Piccadilly, by every worked-out toiler that plunges into the canal. The food this managing class eats, the wine it drinks, the shows it makes, and the fine clothes it wears, are challenged by eight million mouths which have never had enough to fill them, and by twice eight million bodies which have never been sufficiently clothed and housed.

There can be no mistake. Civilization has increased man's producing power an hundredfold, and through mismanagement the men of Civilization live worse than the beasts, and have less to eat and wear and protect them from the elements than the savage Innuit in a frigid climate who lives today as he lived in the stone age ten thousand years ago.

CHALLENGE

I have a vague remembrance
Of a story that is told
In some ancient Spanish legend
Or chronicle of old

It was when brave King Sanchez
Was before Zamora slain,
And his great besieging army
Lay encamped upon the plain.

Don Diego de Ordenez
Sallied forth in front of all,
And shouted loud his challenge
To the warders on the wall.

All the people of Zamora,
  Both the born and the unborn,
As traitors did he challenge
  With taunting words of scorn.

The living in their houses,
  And in their graves the dead,
And the waters in their rivers,
  And their wine, and oil, and bread.

There is a greater army
  That besets us round with strife,
A starving, numberless army
  At all the gates of life.

The poverty-stricken millions
  Who challenge our wine and bread,
And impeach us all as traitors,
  Both the living and the dead.

And whenever I sit at the banquet,
  Where the feast and song are high,
Amid the mirth and music
  I can hear that fearful cry.

And hollow and haggard faces
  Look into the lighted hall,
And wasted hands are extended
  To catch the crumbs that fall

And within there is light and plenty,
  And odours fill the air;
But without there is cold and darkness,
  And hunger and despair.

And there in the camp of famine,
  In wind, and cold, and rain,
Christ, the great Lord of the Army,
  Lies dead upon the plain.

                    LONGFELLOW